Identity Crisis:
Teaching in Higher Education
in the 21st Century

Identity Crisis:
Teaching in Higher Education in the 21st Century

Liz Marr

Rachel Forsyth

Trentham Books

Stoke on Trent, UK and Sterling, USA

Winner of the IPG DIVERSITY Award 2010

Trentham Books Limited
Westview House   22883 Quicksilver Drive
734 London Road   Sterling
Oakhill   VA 20166-2012
Stoke on Trent   USA
Staffordshire
England ST4 5NP

First published 2011

British Library Cataloguing-in-Publication Data
A catalogue record for this book is available from the British Library

ISBN: 978 1 85856 467 8

Designed and typeset by Trentham Books Ltd and printed in
Great Britain by Berforts Group Ltd.

Contents

Acknowledgements

The authors would like to express their gratitude to current and former participants, both staff and students, on the post-graduate Academic Practice programme at Manchester Metropolitan University. Their commitment and enthusiasm inspired us to embark on this project and we hope that they and others like them will find our book helpful.

Particular thanks are due to Professor Janet Beer, for encouraging us to begin the book and agreeing to write the foreword, to Gillian Klein of Trentham Books for her immense patience in editing the results, and to Anna Rose-Adams for checking the typescript so carefully. All remaining errors are, of course, our own.

Preface

Professor Janet Beer

Vice Chancellor, Oxford Brookes University

The character of the academic role is constantly subject to change – as the many and various demands of teaching, research and administration move in tune with the imperatives of the moment – whether as a result of individual career or larger policy decisions. As I write, in October 2010, the Coalition government has just announced policy changes that will conclusively alter the balance of contribution between private and public funding of a university education. If their plans are enacted then the only public funding for university teaching will be in a premium which recognises the additional expenditure required for delivery of the STEM disciplines. The shift for all students to the payment of a much greater contribution will concentrate the minds of students and academics alike about the nature of the academic offer, the student experience and, crucially, what is often termed 'the value proposition' of higher education. Those who, like me, have spent the majority of their careers working in higher education, are only too aware of the challenges which face new academic staff in UK universities and these challenges will be heightened by the seismic changes about to occur.

Academic staff are not only expected to be masters of their disciplines, to be consummate researchers, efficient administrators and sympathetic student counsellors but they must do all these things in an atmosphere where the value of higher education will be under new and often uncomfortable scrutiny. The changes to funding will alter the higher education environment, as will further developments in technology and the injunction to pay attention to student employability; we will also need to be especially vigilant to ensure that higher education remains open to all those with the capacity to benefit. It is not that change in higher education is something new: it has been, some would say, our constant companion, certainly over the course of my own career in local government and in higher education. The removal of the binary divide in 1992, the year in which many of the class of 2010 were born, the introduction of the Research Assessment Exercise and the National Student Survey, new courses on teaching in higher education, the removal of grants and the introduction of fees, the signing of the Bologna accord – to name but a few – have dramatically altered the landscape. Approaches to academic management have also undergone significant changes, as have the responsibilities and accountabilities of higher education institutions with, probably, further regulation to follow.

In any university the students are, of course, the most important stakeholder group but for the university to fulfil its purpose the students must be enabled to work in partnership with the academic and other staff. As a Vice Chancellor I see this partnership as critical to the success of the university. So the preparation of newcomers to higher education is absolutely crucial in order to prepare colleagues for the complexity and multiple responsibilities of an academic career. The apprenticeship route into academe is still the most frequently trodden path – post-graduate study, research assistantship with a little tutorial work and then a lectureship if things proceed smoothly. Whilst in many institutions academic development is available for these entrants, it is by no means universally provided and for those who come direct from industry or professional practice special induction into the range of academic activity is particularly vital. One of the authors of this book described to me her induction as a new lecturer. She took up post on September 1st and was given a timetable and a couple of syllabi, with advice that teaching would start in three weeks. She stumbled through her first few years with dogged determination, watching, listening and learning. Some excruciating embarrassments and many moments of existential doubt, as well as concern for her students, led to her determination to help others who followed in her footsteps.

In a former role as PVC with responsibility for learning and teaching, I worked, with colleagues, to build the post-graduate academic practice course on which the authors developed their ideas for this book. Its genesis was their realisation that although there were texts available on teaching theory and some useful 'how-to' resources for practice, the contextual information needed to make sense of why some things were necessary was harder to come by.

Only a decade into the 21st century, teaching requirements in HE are hugely different even from those of the 1990s and light years away from the minority participation days of the 1960s. In this book those requirements, and the reasons for them, are clearly and straightforwardly set out. For those who want to know how to prepare lectures and deliver them effectively, make learning from group work more meaningful, develop confidence in assessing students or kick-start a research career there are plenty of suggestions. These are usefully prefaced, in the first half of the text, by a description of the UK sector today, its structure, practices and processes. This focus on academic-related functions within the university is especially useful because it shows the crossing points in the boundaries between the purely academic knowledge production and knowledge dissemination and the supporting roles, where help can be found for the hard-pressed lecturer.

There is, though, another valuable aspect to this book. Increasingly, career paths in academe are becoming more permeable. Academics are moving into management roles and more managers are coming in from outside the sector. This latter group will also find the book of use in helping them to understand the challenges faced by academic staff and allowing them to get to grips with what is an unusual and complex sector. Business acumen may well be an essential tool for the future managers in HE but this is insufficient without knowledge and understanding of the academic role and function and the social, political and economic contexts of universities. So the book is not just of value for early career academics but should also be read by early career HE managers.

The university is, and will remain, despite dramatic changes ahead, a wonderful place to work. It offers a unique environment of creativity, of opportunity and of wonder. I learn something new every day in conversation with my colleagues and our students and, in the face of the challenges of the coming period, we will need constantly to bear in mind the reasons why we wanted to spend our professional lives in the business of inspiration.

October 2010

Introduction

Two big questions drive this book: what precisely do we mean by the term 'higher education' in the 21st century and what is the role of an academic in this context? These two questions are clearly inter-related, but there are so many factors buffeting and re-shaping universities and academics in the UK and further afield that it is often easier to ignore the wood and just panic about being lost amongst the trees.

As 'academic developers' (Handal, 2008) teaching on a post-graduate course for new lecturers in a large modern university, we have become very aware of just how complex it now is to be an academic. Roles in higher education (HE) have become more varied and increasingly specialised, with administration and management becoming more prominent, and with more blurring of responsibilities than was previously the case. At the same time, political ideology, policy developments, economic fluctuations and social change play their part in shaping the context and what we do within it: higher education has changed considerably since the early 1980s. Text books on how to teach diverse student bodies abound, as do more abstracted theorisations of what university is for and what is meant by academic identity. What we have tried to do in this book is to bring the two big questions together in order to provide an understanding of the context in which a 21st century academic operates and all that that entails.

Whilst we are concerned with the bigger picture, we are however very conscious of the need for guidance on how one works within it. How do we deal with large groups of learners with different qualifications, aspirations, experiences, knowledge and understanding? How do we give these students their voice and help them to develop as learners whilst at the same time continuing to develop ourselves as professionals in our sector and in our disciplines? Can we become successful teachers, researchers and administrators and be enterprising without suffering early career burn-out? Will we always have to work evenings, weekends and through our official leave just to tread water?

Sadly, we do not claim to have all the answers, but we do aim to provide tools, examples, illustrations and tips on how to enjoy being an academic and have a life! Of course, for those of us who have only recently experienced HE as a student and enrolled in the ranks as young researchers or associate lecturers the culture shock is not so great as for those who came in ten or more years ago. But as all of us who have made the transition from student to lecturer know, the leap is often very much into the dark. Similarly, for those who obtained their academic qualifications some years ago and have undergone a mid-career change – an increasing number in times of economic downturn and in a sector which wishes to link more closely to the world of work – the journey may not be an easy one. With this book, we hope to ease the transition for new academics into the world of higher education.

So what is higher education?

The history of higher education as we know it today is, surprisingly, a relatively short one. Until the end of the 19th century universities were private and founded on voluntary donations and even into the early 20th century, many institutions came into existence as a result of efforts by local civic, professional and commercial elites. It was only after the Second World War, with the emergence of the welfare state and a public sector, that universities began to be seen as valuable tools to support state objectives, particularly in the areas of science and engineering research. Although it seems that this early part of the new millennium has been a period of very rapid change, the last 60 years have actually seen an accumulation of adjustments and adaptation which in Peter Scott's words, represent a 'creeping nationalisation' (Scott 1995:20).

Scott points to three socio-economic shifts which accompanied the early growth of the HE sector in the UK. These are the democratic revolution brought about by the extension of the franchise contributing to the growth of working-class consciousness, the industrial revolution leading to a need for expert technical skills and the rise of the professional society which heralded the bureaucratic state resulting in new training needs. To take this point further, in the same way as some observers (Bell, 1973; Webster, 1995) have recorded a series of industrial revolutions, it might be argued that these three shifts occur cyclically and have continuously shaped and re-shaped the sector. For example, the extension of the franchise to, and greater freedom for, women coincided with an increase in demand for HE. At the same time, new modes of mass production, increased work management and scientific management of labour brought about new professions and required new skills. A fourth shift might be mapped onto the growth of information and communication technologies; new, more flexible forms of work organisation and an increase in leisure activity. Each phase creates demand for new programmes of study and more research. So the development of the HE sector could be said to be a consequence of continual social, cultural and economic change emerging alongside the development of an economic system which is dependent on the continuous pursuit of new knowledge and skills to achieve competitive advantage.

If we try to make a direct comparison between the university student experience of, say, thirty years ago with that of today we would see change but also continuity. One might choose a timeframe of ten, twenty, or even 50 years. Thirty has been chosen here as it marks the point at which participation began to increase to current levels and presaged the expansion of the sector with the removal of the binary divide between universities and polytechnics in 1992. There are considerable differences in the size and make-up of the student body, from that of thirty years ago, with an increase from 15 per cent of the population to just under 45 per cent today (BIS, 2009). There is a much greater age range, more ethnic diversity and a shift from male dominance to a more equal gender participation. There has also been massive growth in the use of technology in teaching and learning, facilitating more distance and on-line learning. But some fundamental elements of university life remain the same. Lectures, seminars and tutorials are still the principal delivery mechanisms; halls of residence and libraries are still recognisable features of the landscape and freshers' weeks and graduation ceremonies maintain the traditions of the sector. Other fundamental changes include the development of new kinds of courses such as Foundation Degrees and work-based learning Continuing Professional Development (CPD) modules. But if anything, the focus on quality and standards has increased, maintaining the value of UK awards and the classification system has not yet been replaced, despite the introduction of results transcripts.

These changes and continuities beg the question of whether the higherness of higher education is still there; whether the distinction between higher and further education can still be perceived, articulated and effectively measured. It seems to us that the identity crisis we refer to in our title is not just about the diverse range of activities that academics now find themselves tasked with but, more fundamentally, to do with our understanding of the university and its role in contemporary society.

Historically, perhaps the two most well-known conceptions of the university are those proffered by Wilhelm von Humboldt and Cardinal John Henry Newman. The former, writing in the early part of the nineteenth century expressed an idealist view in which teaching and research are closely intertwined and where '*the search for truth should be combined with an ambition to live a correct life*' (Humboldt, 1970). The Humboldtian concept emphasises research and scholarship as essential to teaching, that one depends on the other and personal growth comes through learning. Crucially, this can only happen when there is academic freedom and it is in this context that the student begins an apprenticeship in which the teacher and the taught learn together.

Cardinal Newman also highlights an essential spirituality, describing the university as '*a seat of wisdom, a light of the world, a minister of the faith, an Alma Mater of the rising generation. It is this and a great deal more...*' (Newman, 1854). He argues, however, that its purpose is '*the diffusion and extension of knowledge, rather than the advancement*' (Newman, 1854) and that if research is its object there would be no need for students. Von Humboldt's perception was perhaps more influential in Germany than Newman's in Britain, but many writers have since addressed the idea of the university in an attempt to identify its key features (Graham, 2005; Rowland, 2006).

The modern university in Britain owes much, nevertheless, to successive state interventions. If we look back to the Robbins Report (Committee on Higher Education, 1963), which did so much for the expansion of higher education in the UK, we see here a view of the purpose of HE as:

- instruction in skills for employment
- promoting the general powers of the mind
- advancing learning
- transmitting a common culture and common standards of citizenship

The Dearing Review (NCIHE, 1997) took these and the view of various government departments and refined them, thirty years or so later as:

- to inspire and enable individuals to develop their capabilities to the highest potential levels throughout life, so that they grow intellectually, are well-equipped for work, can contribute effectively to society and achieve personal fulfilment
- to increase knowledge and understanding for their own sake and to foster their application to the benefit of the economy and society

- to serve the needs of an adaptable, sustainable, knowledge-based economy at local, regional and national levels
- to play a major role in shaping a democratic, civilised, inclusive society

The clearest difference between these two is the reference to increasing knowledge and understanding for their own sake – an argument for a research function in universities that does not appear quite so specifically in the Robbins statement of purpose. There is also a call for a much higher level of intellectual engagement and social, political and economic purpose as well as social justice.

As we shall see throughout this text, the legacy of the Dearing Review has been far-reaching and to some extent, transformational. Whether we can perceive, articulate or measure 'higherness', is however still uncertain. What we can say is that higher education is different in a number of ways from what happens in further education. It is not just about the development of skills and competences but about the transformation and growth of the learner which in turn brings about transformation in our communities and societies. The responsibility this places on academics is a heavy one, for if they do not continue to fight for academic freedom, the importance of research and scholarship and the individual growth of students, higher education and all it can do for humanity may atrophy, wither and die.

Why do we need a book like this?

Several years ago, one of us moved to a rural part of the UK, into a very old house which needed significant renovation. Amongst other things, the wiring left much to be desired. The previous occupant, clearly reluctant to spend money on a complete rewiring of the house, simply added more wiring to existing circuits with the introduction of each new electrical requirement. Connections were spliced into wires, through holes drilled in walls, and fastened with insulation tape. Apart from the imminent risk of fire breaking out, the overloading of the system rendered the possibility of a complete power failure almost inevitable. That he lived long enough to die of old age is little short of miraculous!

Of course, it is always difficult and costly to adapt to changing circumstances, especially when certainty is lacking. Without wishing to labour the point, universities have had to react to so much in the last 30 years that there has been a tendency to adapt what is there already, rather than re-think what might need to be done so that the system does not get completely overloaded.

Opening up a system to more than a privileged few, without considering whether the terrain and the guidance provided are appropriate, is bound to have consequences. Yet arguably, we have increased participation but tried simply to fit the additional numbers and the greater diversity into existing systems because it is easier than developing new ones.

Not all readers will agree with us that there is a need for sweeping change in the sector: issues such as post-qualification admission, the revision of degree classification systems, two year fast track degrees and more realistic part-time opportunities with suitable funding arrangements are but a few of the areas which have been vehemently debated. Readers may even doubt whether policy decisions which have impacted on their work and experience have always been right. However, we must work in the here and now and our purpose is to help readers to do so. The fact that we do not choose to critique the direction in which higher education has been going and is moving toward does not indicate blind acceptance that all change is for the good. But knowing the context in which we work and understanding what is required of us can better position us to challenge and influence decision making at all levels.

How is this book going to help?

The book is divided into two sections. Part One – *The context: Higher education in the 21st century* – looks at the ways in which the landscape of higher education in the UK has changed over the last 30 years. Successive policy developments in education have radically transformed the context in which university education is delivered, both in the UK and elsewhere in the world. Workers in HE live in a world seemingly directed by league tables, targets, widening participation, competition at regional, national and international levels, student loans, variable fees, talk of the 'iPod generation' and an increased staff-student ratio.

Part One explores the impact on universities of those policies through an examination of the ways in which the sector and universities themselves are managed and run. We look at the way in which policies and strategies impinge on the experience of both teachers and learners across the sector and outline their origins and implications. Then we present our proposals to support university teachers today. Chapter one describes the UK higher education sector – its current size and shape, how it is funded and what state structures are in place to support it. What we see is that state funding is only a partial – and possibly a diminishing – source of revenue, albeit one which largely determines much of the management functions required in universities. Chapter two asks who actually runs universities, before looking at the way in which they are managed. Our descriptions here are necessarily high-level and generic – we focus on what needs to be done. Every institution will have its own culture and idiosyncratic ways of doing things so readers are recommended to reflect on the specifics within their own place of work.

One of the many consequences of varied funding arrangements and policy directives is the necessity to consider the needs of a highly diverse student body. This goes far beyond the widening participation agenda and encompasses trends towards greater internationalisation of the curriculum, both within the UK and globally through new international partnerships and franchises. Furthermore, the skills agenda requires academics to become more flexible in curriculum delivery, the timeframes over which people now study and the locations in which learning and teaching take place. Thus, in addition to the dichotomy of home-versus-international students, we also have a contrast between new communities of learners and our traditional markets. Whilst technology can make some contribution to managing the change, there are still considerable challenges in meeting the needs of learners in HE today. Chapter three heralds the new students and highlights the characteristics which have implications for our practice.

Throughout Part One, we aim to show how the individual academic slots into the bigger picture. In Part Two, *Working in higher education in the 21st century,* we look at what is expected of an academic in this rapidly changing and complex environment and examine the implications for practice. Each stage of the student lifecycle is considered here, from pre-entry to graduation, but this section puts the academic at the centre, showing how important it is for the individual to engage with all facets of university life. Academic staff who are effective, efficient and enjoying themselves will inevitably enhance the student experience across the board. Each chapter explains how to tackle the responsibilities of the 21st century academic and contains tips for teachers as well as examples and analysis of the latest research and thinking on the different aspects of academic life.

Readers might choose to approach this text in a linear fashion – it is designed to be read in this way. But as we realise that an academic new in post will be seeking some immediate *how-to* advice, Chapter four provides an overview of the academic role and some practical guidance on lecturing, tutorials and marking, and on how to get involved in research and academic enterprise. Subsequent chapters relate specific areas of academic activity to the contexts described in part one of the book. Chapter five provides more detailed advice on working with students, and enhancing quality and associated activities are addressed in chapter six.

Finally, we want to stress that although this book talks a lot about universities and students, it is primarily for and about those *working* in higher education. Our final chapter therefore looks at career development and how the autonomy enjoyed in academic roles can be used to gain experience, try new challenges and pursue personal and professional goals.

Part One
The context: Higher education in the 21st century

1

Higher Education in the UK

This chapter gives a brief overview of the factors which have shaped higher education, particularly in the UK, in recent decades. We accept that for readers, the *how* may be more pressing than the *why*. But it would be remiss to present a text on academic work in the 21st century without saying something about the context in which it takes place. The characteristics of the HE sector in the UK, the policy decisions which influence the funding and remit of universities, and the structures and processes which have been established to audit, monitor and in some cases discipline, institutions all impact significantly on an academic's work, sometimes in ways they are not even aware of.

We therefore begin by describing that context and explaining some of its possible impacts on the sector. Political influences are, however, subject to change, and the sector is still evolving in response to recent economic and political decisions. What we describe here is very likely to change in the near future. Over the last 50 years or so there have been many changes in the sector and since the early 1990s, so many policy shifts in relation to education that anyone could be forgiven for asking the bus to stop so they can get off! We hope that our highlighting the history, politics, economics and philosophy of HE will help academics make sense of what is happening and how it might affect them, and will contextualise future changes.

UK Universities – a potted history

Higher education (sometimes referred to as tertiary education) is non-compulsory and usually undertaken at a university or institution of higher education, although there are some exceptions to this. HE involves teaching, research and outreach activity and results in awards at undergraduate or post-graduate level. The traditional focus of HE is theoretical expertise, but there has been considerable growth of vocational HE beyond the professional vocational areas such as law, medicine and engineering, and particularly in areas of practice, such as child-care or health and into areas such as media or tourism.

The earliest recorded universities were founded on mainland Europe, but Great Britain was not far behind. Oxford and Cambridge Universities (founded in around 1096 and 1209 respectively) were the first in the UK, followed by St Andrews in Scotland (founded in 1413). Medieval institutions took young men to prepare them for the professions – law, medicine and theology. They were seats of learning with close links to the Church, and scholars were held in high regard. Surprisingly though, the origins of the large scale HE system we know in the UK today are relatively recent. Until the end of the 19th century, universities were private and founded on voluntary donations and even into the early 20th century, many institutions were the result of efforts by local civic, professional and commercial elites. As the sector expanded, different types of university began to be grouped together: the ancients, the civics (sometimes further divided into so-called red-brick and second-wave civics) and the plate glass (also known as 'Robbins', after the author of the report which gave rise to them). These universities, created before 1992, were instituted by Act of Parliament or Royal Charter and received Privy Council approval to award degrees. Each institution has its own charter which determines some of the characteristics and structures they enjoy.

Growth in the sector was augmented in the 1960s through a major expansion in the number of polytechnics. These tertiary level institutions focused on applied learning, especially in sciences and engineering and awarded degrees validated by the Council for National Academic Awards. However, in 1992 the binary divide between the polytechnics and universities was removed and polytechnics were given degree awarding powers under an Act of Parliament and became funded directly by central government, rather than through local authorities. Since then more institutes and colleges of higher education have acquired university status although not all, as yet, have post-graduate degree-awarding powers. These institutions are often known collectively as the 'post-92s'. Because the sector is now large, with 166 HEIs, of which 116 have the title of 'University' (Universities UK, 2008), most UK HE institutions belong to at least one of a number of lobby groups which reflect their character and mission. These include:

The Russell Group – named after the London hotel in which the first meeting of this alliance was held in 1994. These twenty universities are research intensive and enjoy high international status. They include the Universities of Oxford and Cambridge and tend to be old and wealthy, generating research income and alumni donations from all over the world.

The 1994 Group – named for its year of foundation, the 1994 group comprises 19 research intensive universities, generally smaller than the Russell Group members, and usually established more recently. Their focus is on excellence in research and teaching, both nationally and internationally.

The Alliance – this used to be the oddly-named Alliance of Non-Aligned Universities and was formally established in 2006. It comprises a mix of pre- and post 1992 institutions (ie former polytechnics which took University title in 1992 and ceased to come under Local Authority control). Alliance members are characterised as the middle sector and have missions which give equal status to research, teaching, enterprise and innovation.

Million+ – so-called because between them they have produced graduates in the millions. Originally the Coalition of Modern Universities, they became the CMU (Campaigning for Modern Universities) before re-launching in 2007 as a think tank which counts many of the newer universities among its members.

Guild HE – the smallest and newest of the lobby groups, Guild HE represents the newer universities and colleges of higher education. It sees itself as a representative body rather than a mission group, alongside UUK (Universities UK) and the AoC (Association of Colleges).

There are also specialist institutions such as Colleges of Art, Conservatoires, Schools of Speech and Drama or Performing Arts which generally do not belong to these larger groupings.

Figure 1.1 contains brief descriptions of four UK institutions, to show the diversity of provision in the UK (see overleaf).

One of the biggest changes in the sector in the last fifty years has been the immense growth, not just in the number of universities but also in the number of students taking courses. Universities in the UK now enrol over 2 million students a year, around 20 per cent of whom are at post-graduate level. The numbers who graduate each year are steadily increasing – in 2008 the figure was 334,890. Additionally, some students take HE courses in Further Education colleges, either through franchise arrangements or as validated providers.

Figure 1.1 Descriptions of UK universities

University of Edinburgh

Founded in 1582, the University of Edinburgh is a member of the Russell group and was the fourth university in Scotland at a time when there were only two in England. It has annual income of more than £500 million of which around 175 million is from research grants and contacts and 15 million comes from endowments and investment. It has three colleges: Humanities and Social Science, Medicine and Veterinary Medicine and Science and Engineering and teaches some 24,000 students of which over 7,000 are at postgraduate level. Entry is competitive and requirements are high, with 70 per cent of its young first degree intake coming from state schools and colleges. It achieved tenth place in the 2008 Research Assessment Exercise (RAE).

Oxford Brookes University

Originating in 1865 as the Oxford School of Art, the former Oxford Polytechnic changed its name on acquiring university status in 1992. A member of the Alliance, it has just under 20,000 students, of which around 5,000 are post graduates. It has eight schools and is well known for its automotive engineering courses and close links with Formula 1. Its annual income is just below £160 million, of which the majority is made up of funding council grants and tuition fee income. Just over 70 per cent of its young first degree intake comes from state schools and colleges and it was placed 68th in the 2008 RAE league tables.

Chester University

The University began life as a teacher training college, originally under the auspices of the Church of England. In 1930, it became an affiliate college of the University of Liverpool which awarded their degrees. In the 1960s it became the Chester College of Education but expanded to teach degree courses, becoming the Chester College of Higher Education. It received taught degree awarding powers in 2003, University status in 2005 and the right to award its own research degrees in 2007. Expansion through acquisition of the Warrington Collegiate Institute gave it a strong regional presence and allowed it to strengthen its nursing and health care provision. It has annual income of around £98 million, mainly from teaching grants and fee income from approximately 15,000 students, of which 97 per cent come from the state sector. It reached 108th place in the 2008 RAE league tables and is not affiliated to any lobby group.

Open University

The Open University, or OU as it is widely known in the sector, was set up by the UK government as a distance learning university in 1969. It is the largest university in the UK, teaching around 180,000 students a year, of which approximately 17,000 are post graduate. Some 25,000 study overseas, either directly, for example as members of armed forces serving abroad, or indirectly through a partner organisation, such as the Arab Open University. All under-graduate students are part-time, most are mature, study from home or in the workplace and are supported by locally-based tutors, high quality course materials and an extensive student support service. In addition to its headquarters in the South Midlands, it has thirteen regional and national offices to provide localised support to tutors and students. A member of the Alliance, it has a total annual income of about £400 million. It is gradually improving its research profile, and reached 41st place in the 2008 RAE.

Figure 1.2: UK University awards

Level	Award	Equivalences	Full-time study period
4	Certificate of Higher Education	Higher National Certificate, National Vocational Qualification Level 4	1 year
5	Diploma of Higher Education	Higher National Diplomas, Foundation Degrees	2 years
6	Bachelor degrees with Honours, Bachelor degrees, Graduate Diplomas, Graduate Certificates, Professional Graduate Certificate in Education.	Level 6 National Diploma	3 years
7	Postgraduate Certificate of Higher Education, Postgraduate Diploma of Higher Education, Masters degrees (eg MA, MSc, MBA, MPhil, MLitt)	Level 7 Diploma	1 or 2 years
8	Doctoral degrees (eg PhD, DPhil, EdD)	Specialist Awards	3 years

The sector offers a range of qualifications from Certificate of HE, through Diploma and Degree to a Doctorate, each requiring some form of examination. Figure 1.2 shows the rank order of university awards in the UK and some of their equivalences.

Since 2009, Colleges of Further Education have been able to apply for Foundation Degree awarding powers. These qualifications were introduced as a means of widening participation, addressing skills shortages and providing HE routes for people in work. They are usually of two years duration and can give progression directly onto the final year of an honours degree. Until 2009, colleges wishing to deliver Foundation Degrees had to have these validated by a university but since then a very few have applied for the right to validate and deliver their own awards. New College, Durham was the first to make such an application although the process of seeking approval is complex and costly.

Universities may also award honorary qualifications to those who have made special contributions, not necessarily academic, to the university, community or society. Honorary graduates are expected to make some contribution to the life of the university and to be a spokesperson for the institution. This practice is not uncontroversial, with students and/or academic staff sometimes protesting against some decisions made by their institutions. In 1985, Oxford University voted against awarding an honorary degree to Margaret Thatcher in protest at her funding cuts for education and in 2007 the University of Edinburgh withdrew the honorary degree it had awarded to Robert Mugabe in 1984.

How is Higher Education funded?

UK Universities have three major sources of funding: government (for teaching and research); international and private student fees; and research and enterprise. Apart from Oxford and Cambridge, alumni donations do not yet form a major component of UK funding, unlike in the USA where this is more common.

Government funding for teaching

UK government funding is channelled through the Higher Education Funding Councils for each of the four nations of England, Scotland, Wales and Northern Ireland. Teaching funding allocations are calculated on the basis of student numbers which are controlled by governments. Universities can enrol as many students as they wish, but they will only receive government funding for the numbers the funding council has allocated to them. Places for students from non-EU countries, for example, are not funded by the government and are charged to the individual at full cost. Home students can be given a place over and above funding council numbers if they, too, pay the full cost of their place and do not apply for government support. Funded home student places are supplemented by the fee contributions students make, which were introduced in 1998, following the Dearing Review of Higher Education (NCIHE, 1997) at a rate of £1000 per year. In 2006, the right to charge variable fees was approved with universities charging between £1,175 and £3,000 per year to UK and EU students.

The allocation of places to universities is determined by the Funding Councils according to the decision of the relevant Secretary of State and his or her indicated priorities. In England and Northern Ireland, these are set out in the Secretary of State's annual funding letter. In Wales and Scotland, the systems are similar, although in Scotland further and higher education are funded through the same body. However, priorities are set by national government.

In England, the actual allocation per student is based on the type of course they are studying, with clinical courses falling into a higher band than arts and humanities programmes. The exact banding is shown in the figure 1.3.

Figure 1.3: Banding for different subject areas

Band	Description	Weighting
A	Clinical practice stages of medicine, dentistry and veterinary sciences	4
B	Lab-based subjects – science ,engineering, medicine etc.	1.7
C	Subjects with lab, studio or fieldwork components	1.3
D	All others	1

(HEFCE, 2008)(HEFCE, 2008a)

In 2008/9 the basic fee rate was £3,964 so an individual student would attract a funding council contribution of :

> £15,856 for Band A
> £6,739 for Band B
> £5,153 for Band C
> £3,964 Band D

A formula is then used, based on an institution's student numbers for the previous year. Roughly, the calculation takes into account the total sum of money available, less assumed fee income.

Other factors in the calculation may vary from year to year. These might include the numbers of students taken from areas with lower than average HE participation – the so-called Widening Participation (WP) premium. Although most of this funding is not ring-fenced for specific purposes, there are headings under which it is expected that money will be spent, such as TESS (Teaching to Enhance Student Success); these headings vary from time to time depending on political imperatives. A fuller description of each of the Funding Councils' funding methods can be found on the relevant web-sites.

In addition to funding council income, universities receive money from the Teacher Development Agency (TDA, formerly TTA) to support teacher education and from the NHS to support the training of health service staff. Other organisations may sponsor students privately, paying fees directly to the institution. However, in response to policy introduced in 2007, universities in England and Northern Ireland will not receive any public funding for students who already hold an equivalent or higher level qualification than the one they wish to study. This has made a considerable difference to the finances of all institutions, but particularly to those such as Birkbeck College and the Open University who specialise in part-time provision. The policy has not been extended to Wales or Scotland.

Tuition fees

In addition to teaching grants from funding councils, universities in England, Wales and Northern Ireland can also charge top up fees. From 1998 to 2006, a means-tested contribution up to £1,250 a year was payable by all home students, in advance of study. But in 2004, legislation was enacted which allowed universities to set their own top-up fees, up to a ceiling which is set annually. In order to do so, universities have to submit an agreement to the Office For Fair Access (OFFA), demonstrating that admission policies are equitable and detailing what bursary support they provide to students from poor backgrounds. Welsh and Scottish students studying in their home country do not pay top up fees, but must do so if studying in any other of the four nations.

Unsurprisingly, almost all universities chose to set their fees at the upper limit, although some kept the price for Foundation years or Foundation degrees at the £1000 level. However, as we write this book, the government is considering whether to lift the current cap on tuition fees with effect from 2012, with sums of up to £9,000 per year suggested. This would, it is argued, create a market for HE both across the sector and across disciplines, as more popular courses or more selective institutions would be able to charge higher fees. If the cap is raised by a significant amount, there is likely to be a much greater range of pricing and bigger differentials in what is offered by institutions. It might also mean that considerably more attention will be devoted to market research and product planning in universities than has hitherto been the case.

Part-time students in HE can be charged whatever fees the university wishes. As the credits they study count towards the number of places the funding councils support, they are usually charged the current undergraduate fee, pro-rata for the number of credits they are studying each year. However, postgraduate students, whether full- or part-time, are usually charged a market rate. Universities are free to grow their postgraduate market as a form of income generation, as they are with international students. In effect, overseas students are paying the full market cost of a university place, currently in the region of eight or nine thousand pounds a year.

Financial support for students

Support for tuition fees and living costs for UK students is provided by national governments through a combination of loans and grants. Loans are made available through the Student Loan Company and cover tuition fees in full for all eligible full-time under-graduate students. Maintenance support is provided through means-tested grants and loans, but does not currently cover the full costs of living. Many students nowadays survive with the help of parental contributions, bank overdrafts and part-time work.

Because universities are only allowed to charge higher fees if they have an Access Agreement in place with OFFA, students from low-income back-grounds will be supported. A statutory minimum bursary (amounting to approximately 10% of the fee charged) must be provided for students who are eligible for a full maintenance grant. Universities are also expected to use a proportion of the additional income drawn from fees to provide an enhanced bursary scheme and students may, in some institutions, receive the equiva-lent of a full fee waiver. There are many cases, however, where these addi-tional amounts are dependent on performance, residence or participation in a pre-entry scheme and are more akin to scholarships awarded on merit.

Part-time students, in comparison, get little financial support and this is only available if they are studying at least 50 per cent of a course. There is an assumption that part-time students are receiving support from their employers but in fact this is only the case for 41 per cent of UK part-time stu-dents (Callender *et al*, 2010). Only 22 per cent receive fee waivers or financial assistance and the remainder are self-funded. If the fee cap rises, these learners may be excluded entirely from higher education.

Funding for research

UK government research funding is made available in two ways – via the relevant funding council, using an assessment of research quality (so-called Q funding), and through the Research Councils. There are seven of the latter, as shown in Figure 1.4, and they provide support for specialist research at pure, applied and strategic levels, in their subject areas. Academics may bid into specific programmes which are identified as priority areas, into rolling research funds or to apply for fellowships. The Research Councils also sup-port post-graduate research by funding doctoral studentships. These are allocated to university departments on a quota system according to the ability of the department to provide the highest quality doctoral training. Additionally, they might run early researcher schemes or seminar programmes for dissemination of research findings. Increasingly, Research Councils are concerned with ensuring that the research they fund has appropriate impact and are therefore beginning to fund follow-on research in which resources are made available to help in the practical application of research outputs.

Figure 1.4: List of UK Research Councils in 2010

Arts and Humanities Research Council

Biotechnology and Biological Sciences Research Council

Engineering and Physical Sciences Research Council

Economic and Social Research Council

Medical Research Council

Natural Environment Research Council

Science and Technology Facilities Council

The Councils also provide access to large research facilities such as the European Organisation for Nuclear Research (CERN) in Geneva, and the Diamond Synchrotron in Oxfordshire, as well as supporting specialist research centres, such as the Rutherford Appleton Research Laboratory or the Roslin Institute.

The work of the Research Councils is coordinated by a cross-council secretariat, known as Research Councils UK (RCUK) which encourages and facilitates cross-council research programmes and provides a common framework for working with the Councils, for instance through a single electronic grant application system.

UK funding council support for research is allocated through institutional block grants which are calculated according to an assessment of research achievements and potential. The Research Assessment Exercise (RAE), as it was known, was first conducted in 1986 and subsequently in 1992, 1996, 2001 and 2008. The purpose of the assessment is to profile institutions according to the quality of their research, in order to inform resource allocation. Submissions are made by universities into different units of assessment (for example, politics, sociology or chemistry), and assessed by specialist panels which consider such factors as whether the research is world-leading, internationally excellent, internationally recognised, or nationally recognised. The submissions are mainly in the form of research outputs, principally peer-reviewed publications, but other esteem factors and the research environment are also taken into consideration.

The 2012 assessment exercise has been re-named the Research Excellence Framework (REF) and differs from the RAE in two ways – its use of metrics in assessing research quality and the requirement to incorporate impact measures. The latter is designed to encourage researchers to consider the social or economic benefits resulting from their work, whilst the concept of metrics is intended to find usable measures, such as numbers of citations, to quantify research quality.

Whatever the process, the outcome provides a proxy by which research funding can be allocated as part of the block grant. The intention is not to fund future research, but to contribute to the cost of infrastructure to provide a platform on which research profiles can be built. The Funding Councils recognise that the money they can allocate is insufficient to fully fund institutional research and expect that universities will bid into other sources to do this, such as research councils or trust funds.

Other research funders

The main additional sources of research income for universities are charitable trusts. The most well-known are the Wellcome Trust, the Nuffield Foundation, the Rowntree Trust and the Leverhulme Trust. Each of these has their own mission and research priorities and, as with the Research Councils, will have both rolling funding and identified programmes of study. Decisions are made by the trustees on the basis of how well research proposals fit with their missions and priorities and provide value for money. There can be a range of difficulties associated with obtaining funding from such sources – primarily that full economic costing (fEC) considerably increases financial requirements. fEC was introduced by Funding Councils to ensure that the overheads and fixed costs of the institutional infrastructure are fully accounted for in all activities undertaken. For example, the cost of running a library, of maintaining laboratories and equipment, of processing human resource requirements, are all contributory expenses in the work of an academic researcher. Even the calculation of those costs has to be paid for! So the costs to charitable trusts of providing funds are increasing and this is compounded in times of economic downturn by reductions in the funds available.

Another significant source of support is the European Union, which has funds available for specific research programmes and for projects which enhance communities in member states, socially or economically. These funds, such as the Framework Programmes, European Social Fund or TEMPUS, tend to require collaboration across member states so that knowledge and benefits can be shared.

Devolution – Wales and Scotland

Responsibility for higher education in Scotland and Wales is devolved to the respective national governments – the Scottish Government and the Welsh Assembly Government. Funding for the sector is delivered through the Higher Education Funding Council for Wales (HEFCW) and the Scottish Funding Council (SFC) respectively. Both bodies distribute funds to meet national priorities but only the SFC funds both the HE and further education (FE) sectors.

National priorities are broadly similar, with a focus on economic, social and environmental sustainability. Widening access, employer engagement, world class research and national language and culture are also included, alongside the recruitment of international students.

In Scotland, the SFC funds 49 colleges and 22 universities. Like Wales, Scotland has huge rural areas and provision tends to be focused in the South of the country. The need for more Northerly support in Scotland for HE was identified as long ago as the 1930s, but it was some seventy years before a solution was found, when the University of the Highlands and Islands Millennium Institute was granted taught degree awarding powers in its own right. This unique form of provision gives local access to a partnership of college and research institutes spread across a wide geographical area, and which also includes a network of learning centres.

HEFCW covers a much smaller area and funds twelve HE institutions. A distinctive feature is the support for Welsh medium provision, with around one in 20 learners studying in this way.

Sectoral Support

Although universities in the UK do receive government funds, they are not entirely dependent on them. In a sense, then, they can act as autonomous organisations, deciding how they spend their money and setting their own strategic direction. However, in order to ensure the quality and standards of UK awards, to support sector-wide activities and to protect the interest of potential and existing students, there is a sectoral infrastructure, comprising bodies to monitor quality, support admissions, collate data, support teaching and learning and inform policy.

University admissions

Admission to universities is managed by the Universities and Colleges Admissions Service (UCAS). The UK operates a pre-qualification system of university admission in which offers are made in terms of the results the student must attain in their level 3 examinations, for example Advanced Level General Certificate of Education ('A' level). All applicants wishing to apply to a UK university submit a single form to UCAS, listing up to five choices of course/institution. Applicants who already hold appropriate qualifications can be made an unconditional offer of a place. The form includes a personal statement and a reference, usually from a teacher, indicating predicted results for that applicant. UCAS send the forms electronically to the chosen institutions, where an admissions tutor decides whether to make an offer. The applicant is relayed this information by UCAS, and must decide which offer to accept and which they will take as a back-up should their eventual grades be insufficient.

If the applicant achieves the required results, the university will confirm the place via UCAS and the applicant must take this up. If they decide they wish to go elsewhere, they must request that the university releases them so they can enter the Clearing process. This usually takes place immediately after the national examination results are released in August each year and is the opportunity for applicants who did not meet their offer, or were rejected during the initial process, to apply for remaining places in the sector.

In addition to undergraduate entry, UCAS also manages the Graduate Teacher Training Registry (GTTR) for admission to teacher training courses for graduates, the UK Postgraduate Application and Statistics agency (UKPASS) and CUKAS, the Conservatoires UK Admissions Service. They carry out research and provide statistical data and report to government, universities and other relevant bodies.

The admissions process is largely an administrative one, but there are points at which academic staff input is needed. Admissions were once mainly dealt with by academics linked to courses or programmes. The role of admissions tutor tended to be given to the newest member of the department, who would pass it on at the earliest opportunity. But increasingly, the process is being centralised and professional admissions staff make decisions according to prescribed criteria. However, there is still an important role for academic staff in deciding on the entry criteria for their courses: the required qualifications and levels and what will be looked for in a personal statement. This requires familiarity with a range of prior educational qualifications as well as an understanding of what might be considered appropriate preparation for the course they are admitting to. For many programmes, especially highly selective ones, an interview or audition may be required, and academics will carry these out themselves.

There are many routes by which students can enter universities – they might, for example, be studying at a partner institution and have progression rights to complete their award. They could gain access through an exchange scheme and attend for a part or all of an academic year. Whatever route students take, academic staff need to be aware of the procedures they should follow in order to ensure that access is equitable and transparent.

Ensuring quality and standards of UK awards

The Quality Assurance Agency was set up to check that universities are meeting their responsibilities in managing their standards and quality. The QAA is an autonomous body which is funded through subscriptions from universities and colleges and through contracts with the Funding Councils. They do not impose procedures, nor do they check the actual quality, but they provide an academic infrastructure which universities use as a guide to ensuring equivalence of their awards with other institutions in the UK and Europe. The QAA conducts visits or audits and publishes reports indicating the confidence that can be placed on an institution's quality assurance procedures and the extent to which they comply with the academic infrastructure.

The academic infrastructure has four main agreed components or reference points. The first comprises a set of frameworks for academic awards, which describe the levels of achievement for different award titles, for example the Bachelors degree or Masters award (see figure 1.2). England, Wales and Northern Ireland have a single HE framework which is compatible with that for Scotland. These are compatible with the framework for qualifications of the European higher education area and also link to other qualification frameworks such as the Scottish Credit and Qualifications Framework (SQCF) and the Credit and Qualifications Framework for Wales (CQFW) as well as for England. Students can therefore be assured that wherever in the UK they achieve their award, it has currency throughout Europe. The frameworks provide descriptors which explain what a holder of the award should be able to do conceptually and what skills they will have. For example, a distinction is made between levels of award which equip learners with the skills to exercise some personal responsibility and skills which enable them to make decisions in complex and unpredictable contexts.

The second and related component is a subject benchmark schema. Through this, separate benchmark statements are published for principal subject areas. The list of available disciplines is continually increasing. Each statement indicates the knowledge, skills and abilities students should acquire at threshold, typical and excellent levels. They will also refer to relevant professional requirements, such as the Solicitor's Regulation Authority or the British Psychological Society. The intention is not to impose a national curriculum as such, but to provide guidelines to academics designing courses or programmes of study. So while a student studying Criminology at Sheffield Hallam University may not study an identical curriculum to a student at Salford University, their outcomes in terms of knowledge and ability should be roughly similar.

Programme specifications comprise the third component of the academic infrastructure and the QAA provide guidelines for completing them. Programme specifications are concise descriptions of courses, detailing the intended learning outcomes, the methods of assessment and the levels students should be able to achieve.

Finally, the academic infrastructure contains the QAA Code of Practice. This document sets out good practice in managing quality and standards in relation to ten key issues. These include assessment, programme design, approval, monitoring and review, collaborative partnerships, external examining and work-based and placement learning, amongst others.

The QAA undertakes different kinds of review, but the best known is Institutional Audit. In brief, this necessitates the production of a self-assessment document in which the institution presents a commentary on all existing processes and procedures designed to support the implementation of the academic infrastructure. The QAA auditors will wish to see this, plus the evidence to support its claims in the form of paper trails (minutes from meetings, course handbooks, admissions policies, for example). They will also conduct panel interviews with staff and students before reaching a judgement. The process is peer-reviewed: the panel is made up of experts from HE institutions and the professions.

Other types of review include Collaborative Provision Audit in which partnership arrangements are scrutinised, Integrated Quality and Enhancement

Review which reviews the delivery of HE in further education colleges and Access to Higher Education which reviews Access validating agencies, such as the Open College Network.

Another important function of the QAA is to advise the Privy Council on applications for degree awarding powers. An institution can only be granted the power to award degrees by Act of Parliament or Royal Charter and it is an offence to attempt to award a degree in the UK without proper authorisation. Applications for university title or to award degrees are submitted to the Privy Council who refers them onto the relevant minister, who in turn requests advice from the QAA. After appropriate scrutiny a recommendation is made via the minister to the Privy Council, which then acts on that advice.

Finally, as with other sectoral support institutions, the QAA carries out research and provides specialist support to assist universities in managing and enhancing quality and standards. It works with student support bodies such as the National Union of Students and with the Higher Education Academy (see below) to ensure that all relevant voices are given the opportunity to be heard.

Enhancing student learning in higher education

The QAA are at pains to point out that their role is to ensure that institutions are managing their quality and standards processes adequately. They might check that student feedback in relation to teaching, for example, is followed up and properly dealt with, or that there is a forum for external examiner criticisms to be addressed, but do not comment on methods of delivery or classroom practice unless there were serious concerns evident in the way they were appraised.

The support for teaching, learning and assessment at sector level is provided by the Higher Education Academy (HEA) and an associated network of 24 discipline-based subject centres. The HEA operates across the four nations and like the QAA is funded by institutional subscription, funding council grants and contract income. Its original incarnation was as the Institute for Learning and Teaching in Higher Education which was established in 2000, following the Dearing Review of Higher Education. In 2004, it merged with the Learning and Teaching Support Network (LTSN) and the Teaching Quality Enhancement Fund (TQEF) National Coordination Team (NCT) to become the Higher Education Academy.

Its role is to support the sector as a whole through helping individual academics in delivering a high quality learning experience for students. In addition to hosting seminars and conferences on learning and teaching, the

HEA provides resources and workshops for disseminating good practice, funds research and rewards excellence through the National Teaching Fellowship Scheme. Most significantly, it accredits institutions' Continuing Professional Development (CPD) programmes against the UK Professional Standards Framework for Teaching and Supporting Learning in Higher Education (UK PSF). Academics may achieve HEA recognition though following an accredited programme or submitting an application which shows how they meet the requirements of the UK PSF.

The subject centres provide similar kinds of support for academics and institutions – but with a disciplinary focus. This structure recognises the significance of disciplinary content for teaching, support for learning and assessment, and provides space for academics to collaborate with and learn from colleagues working in the same, or cognate, subject areas in different institutions. With reductions in public funding already affecting the UK, the future of the HEA and the subject centres is uncertain but many academics have benefited from having a forum in which to share practice and learn from each other.

Higher Education and Future Directions – political and economic drivers

The Dearing Report

The status of universities in the UK is unusual in that they are neither completely public nor entirely private sector organisations. Nevertheless, the shape of the sector is very much a consequence of government policies and drivers. We therefore discuss some of the most significant events in recent history which impact on academic work and careers in the early part of the 21st century.

The name of Ron Dearing holds special significance, as it is his review which has done most to shape the HE sector in the UK as it is today. The Dearing Committee was appointed in May 1996 to make recommendations on how the purposes, shape, structure, size and funding of HE, including support for students, should develop to meet the needs of the United Kingdom over the following 20 years. The subsequent report reflected the belief underpinning the investigation that for improved quality of life in the UK for the following 20 years, we needed to develop what Dearing termed 'a learning society'. This would require breaking down boundaries between vocational and academic study and much greater development of links between universities, businesses, etc and the communities they serve. In this way, it would be possible to:

encourage and enable all students – whether they demonstrate the highest intellectual potential or whether they have struggled to reach the threshold of higher education – to achieve beyond their expectations. (NCIHE, 1997)

The wide-ranging report addressed the role and purpose of universities in relation to contemporary society and the way in which they needed to operate in order to carry out this role effectively. It resulted in perhaps the most fundamental sectoral change since the Robbins report of the 1960s, which expanded the sector with the addition of Polytechnics.

Several outcomes of the report have had a major impact on those working in HE today, most significantly the introduction of fees so that students would make a contribution to the increasing cost of their courses. The report suggested that academic pay had not always kept pace with other professions, but that any review had to take into consideration the broader context of affordability as well as conditions of service and work practices. It was this recommendation which paved the way to the introduction of the framework agreement which now governs academic pay and conditions across the UK.

Widening participation received considerable attention in the report, and recommendations included the proposal that Government consider funding strategies which encouraged institutions to support non-traditional students to access and progress through higher education. It advocated a doubling of the Access funds made available to institutions and enhanced support for disabled students. However, future expansion of HE provision was explicitly confined to sub-degree level awards, namely Foundation degrees.

As well as Programme Specifications, progress files which would document a learner's achievement and allow students to monitor, reflect and build on their personal development, were recommended. Other proposals concerned quality assurance, business spin-offs, diversity of mission – almost every aspect of higher education is addressed in the 93 recommendations, including a proposal that the state of the sector be reviewed every ten years. It is worth reading at least the summary of the report and recommendations to get a thorough picture of the sector.

Skills and the economy – the Leitch report

Although not directly focused on higher education, Lord Sandy Leitch's report, *Prosperity for all in the Global Economy – World Class Skills*, (Leitch, 2006) had a major impact on UK policy for HE. The most frequently quoted statistic from the report is that, when it was written, 70 per cent of the working age population of 2020 had already left compulsory education. When related to the report's recommendation that in excess of 40 per cent of the population should be qualified at Level 4 and above, the implications for universities became clear. More effort would need to be targeted at adult learners, probably in the workplace and through engagement with employers. Devising ways of making such provision available has been high on university agenda ever since and new partnerships, with Lifelong Learning Networks, Sector Skills Councils and Regional Development Agencies have added to the complexity of external engagement.

The Leitch report also stressed the importance of raising skill levels among younger learners, including in literacy and numeracy at General Certificate of Secondary Education level (age 16) and encouraging young people to stay in some form of education or training until at least the age of 18. The 14-19 Diplomas, new qualifications which combine vocational and academic approaches and better prepare young people for university in professional and vocational subject areas, were also identified as of utmost importance in this context. For universities this means not just looking at progression routes for apprentices but also working with schools and colleges to ensure that the content of the new diplomas is appropriate for admission to HE.

The European context – the Bologna process

The UK system of higher education does not exist in a global vacuum – it is part of something much greater. Although some of the UK's most respected institutions were amongst the earliest in existence, mainland Europe is acknowledged as the birthplace of higher education and the leader in subsequent developments. In the UK, there is a form of mixed economy where some powerful institutions are able to resist the domination of funders, whereas in Europe the state has more control over public universities and academics are often civil servants. In some cases accreditation of programmes is conducted by government ministries and staffing issues determined by regional or national governments rather than by individual institutions, as in the UK.

It is within this context that the Bologna process, based on the 1998 Sorbonne declaration of an intention to harmonise the European higher education system, was signed in 1999 by 29 European countries (European Education Ministers, 1999). The intention was to create a higher education framework (the European Higher Education Area or EHEA) across Europe in which a comparable system of under- and post-graduate degrees using a common credit system would enhance student and staff mobility and thereby employability and international competitiveness. Education ministers have met annually since then to discuss progress, and 46 countries are now involved in the process.

A major challenge presented by Bologna concerns the length of time deemed appropriate for achievement at Bachelors, Masters and PhD levels. Most continental European universities offered five year programmes culminating in a Masters level award, whereas in the UK a three year undergraduate programme can be topped up with a one year masters. Issues of quality, governance and standards are still only partially resolved and it has been claimed that the 2010 implementation deadline was optimistic, with 2020 being a more realistic target.

Conclusion

The context of higher education work is complex. Even within the UK, there are differences in approach among the four nations. Attempts to harmonise with Europe add to the challenges for academics, administrators or managers in universities and colleges. This chapter has provided an overview of the sector, highlighting the elements which will affect our day to day experience in some way.

Although universities are autonomous institutions, they are required to interact with a number of other agencies and operate within the broader framework of the education system. Knowing how students come to us, how they are supported financially, and what the qualifications they study for actually represent, enables us to support the student experience and better to understand the roles of others who work in universities.

Funding is clearly critical – it can fundamentally affect the mission, structure and function of our institutions. It also constrains the ways in which universities can be run – a matter we consider in Chapter two.

2

The 'new' university

This chapter explores the management of universities in the context
of the HE sector as described in the previous chapter.

What are universities and what are they for?

Deciding what a university is is probably easier than trying to reach agreement on what it is *for*. Like most organisations, universities comprise a collection of people and buildings linked by a common purpose. The objective of the university is the production and dissemination of knowledge. The knowledge might be sought for its own sake – for example, to better understand the world in which we live – or it might be for a specific purpose – perhaps to find an antidote for a newly identified virus.

The use to which this knowledge is put is not always within the control of the university but they are seen as having a public role which manifests in the ways in which knowledge is disseminated. This might be through the publication of books or articles; the presentation of ideas in public lectures or at gatherings of others working in the same field; through feeding into public policy or professional practices; and through teaching.

Universities are quite distinct from both public and private sector organisations in their *modus operandi*. They receive public funding and are therefore expected to support national priorities and meet externally set regulatory and quality standards. Nowadays they also have to generate additional income to support the objectives expressed in their mission statement. They are free to develop spin-off companies or businesses, sell their knowledge and expertise in the open market, recruit students from overseas or receive philanthropic donations. Their functions and structures are therefore many and complex, and some may even seem to be superfluous or unnecessary to the academic staff.

Who runs universities?
State or national government?

David Watson has described universities as occupying a 'peculiarly hybrid world of public-private ambiguity' (Watson, 2008). Since a key source of funding for most UK universities is, at present, the public purse, distributed through the Higher Education Funding Councils for England, Scotland and Wales, and the Department of Education for Northern Ireland, the Funding Councils effectively act as buffer bodies between government and the sector, and advise the minister responsible for higher education on funding needs. They also act as regulators in securing quality and controlling supply and demand, and establish stakeholder confidence in the sector. However, whilst the funding councils might be able to influence state decisions, these are largely a result of government policy which determines perceived needs and how to address them. This is apparent in the decision made in 2010 to raise the cap on the student fee contribution to £9,000 while simultaneously re-ducing state contributions to costs. This was strongly protested by present and future students and academics but was still voted through in Parliament, albeit by a greatly reduced majority.

Policy decisions are, however, made mostly on the back of research, consulta-tion and recommendations. The Funding Councils are active in commission-ing these, contributing to the debates and representing the interests of the Institution. In this respect they have to manage a delicate balancing act, espe-cially as the interests of a Russell group university may be diametrically opposed to those of, say, a Million+ member. One way in which this is achieved is through the use of the formula funding described in Chapter one, which determines the block grant which universities 'are free to spend according to their own priorities within our broad guidelines' (HEFCE, 2008). Whilst institutions are accountable to the Funding Councils and, ultimately, to their national governments for the way they use funds, the formula approach is designed to minimise the burden of accountability since institu-tions are quasi-independent bodies and are free to raise money from other sources. Nevertheless, the majority of UK HEIs currently depend on Funding Council support for at least 30 per cent of their funding, with tuition fee income generating the second biggest proportion.

Thus public funding brings public accountability and the Funding Councils provide a framework for this in their annual reporting requirements. They do so not to control and direct the sector, but to maintain it in such a way as to produce assurances for all the investors in UK HE and to maintain the reputa-tion of each university and the sector as a whole. Importantly, this supports the generation of alternative sources of income for the sector, particularly in the form of commercial research funding and overseas student recruitment. The HE sector is said to be worth in the region of £45 billion to the UK economy and so it is vital to ensure that its reputation remains intact in the face of new competition from the global education market. Internationally, the level of education is perceived to be directly related to a country's economic performance: 'New university graduates indicate a country's capacity to absorb, develop and diffuse knowledge and to supply the labour market with highly skilled workers' (OECD, 2009:16). That the French, German and American governments are at present considering huge injections of capital to their universities indicates how important they believe their HE outputs to be for economic health and competitiveness.

Thus the picture is of some control but very little compulsion, other than economic drivers which operate through 'a 'bid and deliver' system of public funding in the UK which has seen financial allocations tied to tightly specified performance' (Becher and Trowler, 2001:7). These authors point out, however, that as state funds have dried up (or at least reduced), universities have been forced to search elsewhere for funding. The increased marketisation of the sector observed by writers (Slaughter and Leslie, 1997; Becher and Trowler, 2001) could be said to be part of state strategic planning for the sector in which it seeks to reduce its financial responsibilities whilst maintaining a role in ensuring quality and thereby market value. In the words of a former English Minister for Higher Education:

> If we don't get many more people at all levels to higher levels of skills and qualifications, then we are fundamentally going to lose out in terms of economic competitiveness. To face up to that, you need a cultural change, you need the Government to be committing, you need individuals and employers to be contributing. (Attwood, 2007)

Ironically – or perhaps as the result of planning – whilst universities might strive to act as private sector organisations and become self-reliant, this will be achieved principally through their attempts to meet government strategic objectives: delivering world class education, training and research, but at minimal cost to the state.

Universities or university managers?

Governments could therefore be said to run universities. However, the instruments used to establish universities complicates the picture. Chapter one noted the two principal means by which UK universities have acquired their status: by Royal Charter or by Act of Parliament – in both cases approved through the Privy Council. Effectively, these processes restrict the ability to offer a degree level qualification to an approved set of organisations, but they also impose a statutory requirement for governance, mainly through a board of trustees or governors.

In Chartered institutions, decision making is carried out by a Senate, comprising key members of the university, including students and lay partners. In newer institutions, the equivalent body is the Academic Board. Their role is to agree on the awards to be offered, the entry requirements for students and the way in which teaching and research are organised. The difference between these two approaches to governance and management is illustrated by the two examples shown in Figure 2.1 opposite.

Whether it is the governors, the academic body or a senior management team running the university depends on a whole range of factors, such as the make-up of the governing body, the strength of personality of the Chair of governors, the approach of the vice-chancellor, or the culture within Senate or Academic Board. There is a general perception that newer universities are managed by the VC and his or her executive team whilst in older institutions the academic committees wield greater power. In both cases, the governors or trustees are expected to approve the strategic direction of the institution, ensure financial probity and the integrity of its awards. However, it is the vice-chancellor and the finance director who are responsible to the Funding Councils for reporting on spending and results and it is more common in all types of UK institution for these two to have the ultimate say in how the university goes about its business.

The way in which universities are managed, as opposed to run, is addressed in the next section but first we consider what is entailed in running a university. Essentially, this includes setting strategic direction, ensuring that income and expenditure balance favourably and reacting to sudden changes in the wider environment.

Strategic planning in universities is a relatively recent innovation. It requires decisions to be made about the direction the institution should take, for example, to focus on research, teaching or both; move into international markets or develop community engagement. It also comprises activities like horizon scanning: seeing what is likely to come up in terms of policy change, funding sources, demographic shift or economic downturn. The estate must be reviewed – are the buildings fit for purpose? Are they costly to maintain;

Figure 2.1: Comparison of institutional governance and management structures

New Student University is a very large former polytechnic which acquired university status as a result of the Further and Higher Education Act 1992. Its Board of Governors has 21 members, including the vice-chancellor (VC), two co-opted staff and two student members. The other members are mainly lay, apart from a VC of a neighbouring university and a local college principal (also co-opted) and an Academic Board nominee. Governors are selected through advertisement and interviewed by the VC, the Chair of Governors and a member of the nominations committee. The University Registrar is secretary and clerk to the governors. The role of this governing body is to ensure accountability and probity and to protect the public interest.

The university is managed by a team headed by the vice-chancellor and the Executive, comprising two deputy VCs, the Registrar, and Directors of Finance, Human Resources and Services. They meet fortnightly, alternating with the Directorate meeting, which is made up of the Executive and the Faculty deans (who are also pro-vice-chancellors with cross-institutional roles) and heads of services. Interaction between these groups and the governing body is through the VC and the Registrar, although Governors hold strategic planning 'away days' twice a year, to which the Executive are always invited and the Directorate occasionally.

The role of the Academic Board, which is chaired by the VC and comprises directorate, heads of academic departments and members nominated by Faculty boards, is to bring into existence the academic elements of the university's strategic objectives through ratification of new awards and regulations. The Board is 'supported' by a committee structure but any suggested activity is allocated to project groups which are formed only if the Directorate agree they are necessary and can be implemented within the existing resource base.

Old Student University is a large Russell group university which received its Charter and associated statutes, ordinances and regulations which determine the way the institution is managed in the 19th Century. The Charter requires the appointment of a Board of Governors which 'shall be responsible for the custody and use of the Common Seal'; a Senate which, like New Student University's Academic Board, is the academic authority but has greater autonomy; and a General Assembly which represents the university to its community and has the authority to express views and opinions which the Board is required to consider.

The Board has 24 members of which 14 are 'lay'; six are members of Senate; two are non-teaching staff representatives nominated by the General Assembly; and the Vice Chancellor or President and the General Secretary of the Students Union are ex-officio members. The Senate has 64 members, mainly nominated from the School Boards, and the General Assembly has over 150 members which include a range of staff, lay and public sector representatives. Membership of each group is fairly tightly prescribed, suggesting less autonomy for the university's senior management in determining strategy and direction. Thus, whilst the Board is responsible for the strategic direction of the university, the Senate is responsible for keeping this under review in their determination of the academic activity of the university.

does equipment need updating; will they still be appropriate in the next ten or twenty years?

The biggest element of expenditure in any university is the staff budget. The profile of the academic body has to be right for the curriculum the university wants to deliver, and that in turn has to be appropriate for the population the university is serving. Academic functions are only part of the human resource requirements; the staff must include people who support students, carry out administration, maintain the buildings, and provide food and accommodation. In some institutions, where significant library or museum collections are held, for example, specialist staff are also required.

So running a university is about more than just what the institution wants to do – it is also about how it gets it done. Funding bodies may set constraints according to government requirements, but the need to generate other sources of income and balance the books means that institutions have to operate almost as private sector bodies within the public sector. Whether we think this is right or wrong does not obviate the need for decision making at a strategic level. The extent to which this impacts on academic staff, or allows their input, is part of the matter of how universities are managed.

Managing universities

The way in which a university is managed is, as with any large organisation, tied to its objectives and functions. The primary functions of teaching, research and academic enterprise may well be delivered by academic staff but they are usually supported by an administrative body. Unusually though, the lines of command tend to be separated out into a dual line management system – academic and administrative – with possibly somewhat more management on the administrative than the academic side. This section looks at the key functions of the University and how it is supported administratively and managerially. Breaking these down by the core activities creates some difficulties when we try to incorporate core functions which don't come directly under the headings of teaching, research or enterprise, such as student recruitment, financial management, accommodation. These might not be the direct concern of academic staff, but knowing what is going on in the institution and how it impinges on an academic's daily life is crucial to being a successful and happy academic.

We focus on the key output of a university – knowledge – and how it is disseminated to its public. First, however, we offer an overview of its functionality and how this is managed through committee structures and governance.

Figures 2.2 and 2.3 (overleaf) show ways in which management and committee structures might be organised in a typical UK university. These vary from institution to institution – for example, there may be additional functions which are not shown here or they may be managed in different ways – but the figures do give a flavour of how much needs to be considered in the running of a university.

Working with students
Teaching

Teaching as a means of disseminating knowledge seems an obvious place to start, but there is far more to the process than just delivering pearls of wisdom. Programmes have to be designed, courses written, syllabi and assessment agreed and all these have to be approved. Part two of this book devotes more time to these practicalities: here we consider the organisational context and the support needed to ensure they are achieved.

Most of us work in universities which have established programmes of study. They might be specialist institutions focusing on a narrow range of courses, such as agriculture, art or drama; research-intensive science-based colleges; or they may cover the whole gamut of disciplines. The decisions about what subjects to offer are usually based on historical specialism, market and industry demand and forecasting of new areas of growth. However, financial considerations are also extremely influential. For example, in the UK in the late 1990s and early 2000s, criminology began to be offered by some Social Science or Sociology departments. Demand for places shot up, often displacing the sociology courses from which they had sprung and becoming, in some instances, departments of study in their own right. On the other hand, subjects such as languages and physics struggled to recruit, leading many departments to merge with others or close completely. Some institutions chose to concentrate on the delivery of flexible, employer-based programmes whilst others looked to future-proof their provision by moving into specialist areas. The University of Portsmouth, for example, has used its coastal location as a driver for developing a marine-related curriculum, offering courses in marine biology, marine sports technology and marine environmental science.

Economic factors also influence what can not be offered. If a university anthropology department, for example, fails to recruit sufficient students to justify keeping staff employed, managers will be urged to redeploy those staff elsewhere and close the department. The options, then, for the anthropology lecturers are to find new ways to recruit students, try to bring in more research income or to re-focus their curricula.

Figure 2.2: Management structure of a typical UK university

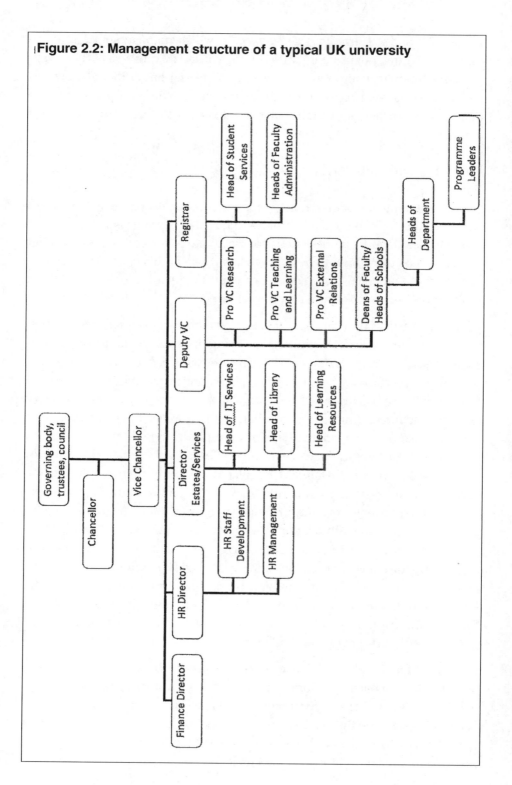

Figure 2.3: Committee structure of a typical UK university

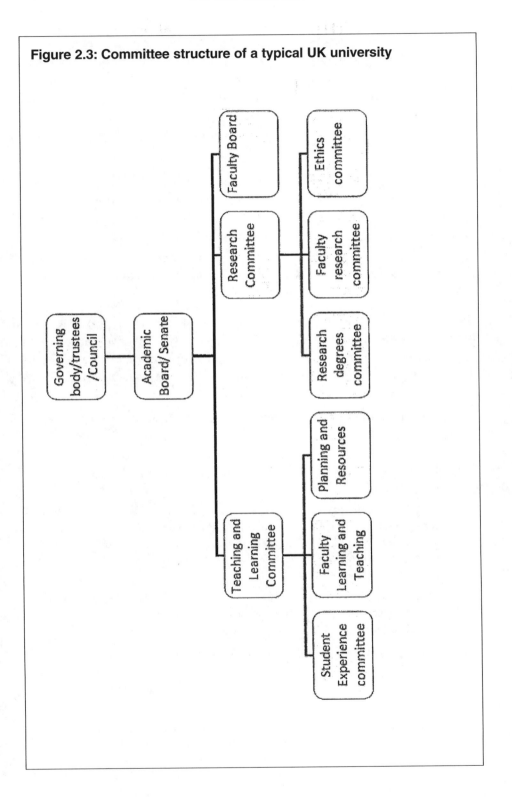

For most UK universities, especially when economic drivers are now so significant, it is vital to keep the curriculum offer under review. In some instances, governments will try to support at risk areas they believe to be important for national competitiveness. In the late 1990s, mathematics and sciences fell into this category but were maintained despite their lack of popularity and continue to be so, through the provision of extra funded places and other incentives.

There are, then, many considerations to take into account when deciding on the size and shape of a curriculum. Careful planning and approval processes are needed, to ensure that what is offered and delivered is appropriate, and also that the institution can deliver it effectively. It is of no use to move into the field of new materials for the aircraft industry if the appropriate laboratory and workshop space is not available. Nor would it be sensible to offer a course of study if there is no expertise in the institution to design and deliver it.

Once the planning stage is worked through, the writing and quality assurance processes come into play. Figure 2.4 shows a typical development and approval process. These vary from institution to institution but quality standards, as we saw in Chapter one, are laid down at national level and must be

---

Figure 2.4: Course development and approval process for a typical UK university

1. **Strategic approval (at university level)** – does it fit with university strategy? Can it be resourced? Is there a need/demand?

2. **Submitting the case (at faculty/school level)** – what is the academic rationale? What is the market demand like? Can the school or faculty provide resources to teach it, including staff, library, IT, other equipment and space. Where will the additional student numbers come from? What career prospects will students have? What is the proposed programme content and structure?

3. **Preparing for scrutiny (at programme level)** – production of the definitive document, programme specification, syllabi etc with focus on teaching and learning, assessment, student support, monitoring and review arrangements.

4. **External scrutiny (at university level)** – one or two external assessors and at least one internal assessor from another part of the institution. Review of documentation and questioning of course team, resource holders and existing or potential students/ partners.

5. **Outcomes** – Approval for a period of time (usually five years), approval with conditions, approval with recommendations, referral for further development work.

---

adhered to in order to ensure parity across the sector. (This process, and how academic staff engage with it, is discussed in Chapter six)

Supporting teaching – Academic developers

Deciding on what is to be taught and how is only part of the process. Ensuring you have the human resource to deliver it is equally critical. New programme proposals generally emerge from academic staff with an interest in or enthusiasm for the subject to be taught. They will have the disciplinary knowledge and expertise of a subject specialist and are also likely to have some experience in teaching. Not all academics, however, will have teaching qualifications: some may have come into universities from industry or practice, whilst others may find themselves feeling out of touch with developments in teaching and learning, especially the use of new technologies.

Many universities will have a department or centre which provides support for the design and delivery of learning, teaching and assessment. This centre may be responsible for delivering the institution's Academic Practice qualifications, supporting the development of e-learning or introducing initiatives such as embedding employability, designing out plagiarism or integrating personal development planning.

Work in centres such as these has been greatly assisted by the activities of the Higher Education Academy (see Chapter one) and its associated subject centres. It has also been influenced, at least in England, by the Centres for Excellence in Teaching and Learning. In 2005, 74 such Centres were established with HEFCE funding, ranging from Active Learning in Computing at the University of Durham to the School of Oriental and African Studies' Languages of the Wider World. Research from the UK-wide Teaching and Learning Research Programme (TLRP) has also impacted on the work of academic developers, in their role as conduits of new thinking into institutions.

Recruiting and admitting students

Once a programme has been approved, it needs to be marketed and students recruited to it. The usual way of reaching potential markets is through the printed university prospectus, although nowadays would-be students more frequently access an on-line version. Although a marketing department or similar will be responsible for pulling the information together and publishing it, academic staff need to provide the description of the course, decide who it is suitable for and what special features there might be, such as a work placement, a year abroad or the opportunity to study a language, and what graduates might go on to do.

The department responsible for recruitment and admissions will take this information out to higher education fairs, school events and other fora at which young people, adult returners, careers advisers, teachers and parents gather to conduct their own research. Such is the level of provision in the 21st century that competition between UK universities for students is strong both at home and internationally, and any opportunity to flourish the brand is worth taking.

Another important function is the organisation of Open or Visit Days, which are now an essential element of the university calendar as much for parents as for their children. Potential students want to visit the department and find out about the course they are planning to study, but are also keen to see the accommodation and facilities, so organising events centrally helps to achieve economies of scale. The use of students as ambassadors on the day is also common-place with recruitment, training and, sometimes, payment all managed centrally. Academic involvement in these events is usually in putting on exhibition lectures or sample tutorials and being available to answer detailed questions about the courses on offer.

Recruitment departments also have expertise in gathering relevant market intelligence. They can tell, for example, which schools and colleges generate the most applications to the university, which faculties or departments those applications are most likely to go to and which convert well into student numbers. Equally, they can tell which are the potentially good, but currently underactive, sources. This kind of data is invaluable to academic staff as it can help to decide where recruitment efforts should be focused and whether closer relationships should be sought with specific feeder institutions.

The admissions department, often attached to recruitment and in some cases linked to marketing, is responsible for processing applications. We saw that all applicants have to go through UCAS (the University and Colleges Applications Service) which does everything from receiving application forms to issuing final confirmation of a place. The university admissions processing staff will receive the UCAS forms, record them on a database, send them to the appropriate department for an admission tutor to make a decision and then process that decision. Once the student's qualification results become available (usually in mid-August) the admissions tutor will confirm or reject the applicant and the admissions department relays this to UCAS, who informs the student.

The point at which results are received and places confirmed is a time of considerable activity, as students who did not attain the grades for their first or second choice of university scramble to find a place elsewhere. Universities themselves use this Clearing period to fill courses on which there are still places. The matching process takes place ostensibly over the few weeks up until the beginning of the academic year (usually September) but in fact is usually completed within two or three days. This complex procedure was once managed by admission tutors but is now the focus of frenetic activity in call-centre style clearing houses managed by Recruitment and Admissions departments. The importance of academic admissions tutors' input cannot be overstated. Students recruited during Clearing are reputedly the most likely to drop out of courses, so the matching process has to be given careful consideration, if it is to benefit both parties.

In many universities the recruitment and admission functions are now centralised – standard offers are agreed with departments and made to suitable applicants. The admissions function has been professionalised, with specially trained staff able to take decisions based on personal statements and teacher references. University admission has also become increasingly complex because of the number and variety of possible entry qualifications. In England, these range from traditional Advanced level General Certificate of Education (GCE) through BTEC vocational awards to Access to Higher Education courses. There is also an increasing number of applicants with Scottish Highers, and Irish Leaving Certificates, not to mention the European Baccalaureate and other international qualifications.

Recruitment of international students is slightly different and is usually undertaken by an international department, either directly at international HE fairs or through in-country agents. Competition here is even more intense, mostly between UK universities, but increasingly with other countries which are enjoying a surge in popularity as exchange rates, natural disasters, health pandemics and international terrorism may be as strong an influence as the choice of course or reputation of the university.

Additional factors need to be taken into account, such as the requirements for a minimum level of proficiency in English, the necessity for students to obtain visas and to demonstrate they have sufficient money to pay the fees and support themselves. As international student fees have become such a significant element of non-government funding for UK universities, the importance of overseas recruitment has increased markedly in the early part of the 21st century. But, as we see in Chapter three, the rise in international student numbers heralds increasing pressures for academics in ensuring that courses of study and their content are appropriate and that students are properly supported. The international department can assist here, although a quick scan of university international strategies does reveal a tendency to focus on recruitment markets rather than pedagogy!

Supporting students

Once students have accepted the offer of a place, they need information about when to enrol, what they need to bring, how to get accommodation and how to sort out finance. Packs are usually put together by administrative staff but academic staff may wish to add other kinds of information, such as course handbooks, timetables or study guides. The packs are most commonly distributed during what is known as induction. At one time, this was referred to as Freshers' week and was a chance for students to get involved in the social events organised by the Students Union but nowadays there are also many departmental activities in addition to enrolment – meeting personal tutors, hearing about the services available, getting access to computer networks and finding the way round the library. We offer practical suggestions on pre-entry and induction in Chapter four, but here we look at how these activities are supported by the institution.

Some believe that too much is attempted during a single week of induction and that the process should be stretched out over a longer period. Or that it is not the role of academics to do these things – they are here to teach. But the 21st century university is a different place from that of the mid 20th century and students too are different. It is suggested that 'helicopter' parents have rendered them more dependent and less self-sufficient and that the modern school curriculum deters independence in learning, implying that today's students might need more support than their predecessors with adapting to university life.

This might be why student support and welfare services increased dramatically during the last decade. As well as accommodation services, chaplaincy and counselling services, universities now offer study skills support in generic and bespoke formats. And as we discuss in Chapter three, the impact of legislation and policy decisions have given rise to disabled student services and Access to Learning funds, which have to be managed and delivered.

Working with post-graduate students

As numbers of undergraduate students have increased, those continuing to Masters level, possibly to differentiate themselves in a competitive job market, have also grown. At the same time, the possibility of studying for a PhD has become more difficult as funding sources have dwindled. Most international

PhD students are self-funded whilst home students tend to subsist on studentships and some teaching. Financial support may come from the institution and be 'fees only' or 'fees plus support' or might come in the form of a grant from a research council or an employer. However they come to the institution, they need to be supported through the processes and procedures which govern study at this level.

The objective of post-graduate study is to develop, or begin to develop, new knowledge. But mere registration for a post-graduate course of study is not itself sufficient to proceed. Most institutions require a candidate to have achieved a good degree (upper second or above) and a recommendation from an academic source. At level seven or above there is also a need to ensure that the objectives of the student meet the university's criteria – they need to submit a proposal which demonstrates that the research is feasible, relevant and can contribute to knowledge. Decisions on this are usually taken by a research degrees committee which also approves the supervision, the external examiner, and any requests for extensions, suspension or deferment of study.

Supervision of research degrees is now regulated closely at institutional level. For example, eligibility to act as Director of Studies or external examiner includes serving on supervisory or examination panels. New academics need, therefore, to find opportunities to do this in order to develop their supervisory capacity. These protocols are overseen by committees established to ensure that standards are maintained.

A university's research department will support the committee in ensuring the correct procedures are followed and regulations are adhered to. The department will also provide support to post-graduate students, addressing any complaints and will provide training and advice for supervisors and directors of study.

The relationship between a post-graduate student and their supervisor is very different to that between an under-graduate and their tutor. The post-graduate student may well be working on a research project alongside their supervisor and contributing to their work. They will have more one-to-one meetings but will also spend far more time on their own. For this reason, drop-out is a real risk and research departments orchestrate regular monitoring of progress to promote support and minimise attrition.

Supporting graduates

Another major growth area in academic support has been careers advice. Most institutions have some form of careers department which has traditionally supported graduates in finding employment or going on to further study. In the latter case, their role has usually been to identify possible funding sources and advising on appropriate routes for specific career development. In terms of finding employment, their role has been to feed in information about opportunities, either at milk rounds (a tradition of large employers visiting universities to talk about available vacancies or graduate training schemes), setting up employer visits, or disseminating vacancy details to final year students.

Increasingly though, careers departments are getting involved in the student journey at a much earlier stage. This is partly due to the introduction of Personal Development Planning (PDP) in 2000 and partly to drives to enhance employability of graduates. The push to make graduates more employable comes largely from the perception of universities as sources of skilled workers in the national economy. But complaints from employers that graduates do not have the skills needed, prompted governments to require universities to provide training and support for the development of employability skills.

PDP was one way in which it was believed this could be done. Universities were expected to provide space for students to assess their skills base, plan their career objectives and reflect on their learning. Career departments began to get involved by providing generic and bespoke workshops on CV writing, career planning and employment options. It was anticipated that personal tutors would also be involved in delivery of PDP but, in fact, it was often devolved to student support and careers departments, particularly if it was seen as extraneous to an academic course of study. Advocates of PDP have recently gone rather quiet, as portfolio-building is increasingly seen as a more appropriate means of encouraging students to reflect on their learning. However, some careers departments are still involved in providing modules of study which carry credit and relate to preparing for employment and employability.

As work-related learning and Foundation degrees become more prevalent, careers advisers in universities are often engaged in finding and advertising work-place learning opportunities to student cohorts. Jobs for life are no longer the norm for graduates anywhere and careers departments have to adapt to this and contribute to preparing students for a new world of multiple career changes.

Another important function is the Destinations of Leavers from Higher Education (DLHE) annual survey. Careers departments contact students at periodic intervals after graduation to assess their progress. This exercise was primarily designed as a means of assessing one aspect of a university – the extent to which its graduates are desirable in the market place. But the data is extremely useful for academic departments and is increasingly used as a form of feedback (alongside results, external examiner reports and student survey responses) to inform course design and development.

Generating new knowledge – the research function in the university

As well as supporting work with post-graduate students, a research department will be expected to make a major contribution to the management of the university's research activity. Primarily, this will be by acquiring funding, through identifying sources, assisting in the writing of bids, carrying out costings and obtaining senior management approval for the project to be carried out .

In Chapter one, we outlined the funding opportunities for research in the UK. It is the role of the university's research department to support academic staff in accessing these opportunities. Research department staff have expertise in bid writing and costing but also have a remit to ensure the proposed research or bid fits with the institution's strategic priorities and can be achieved without incurring cost to the university or damage to its reputation.

For early career researchers or those new to academia, the processes can seem confusing and overly bureaucratic. However, competition for research income is fierce and the more support they can be given, the better the chances of success. Academics may also, legitimately, question why income they generate does not come directly to them or their department. As we saw in Chapter one, the costs of running universities, providing laboratory or workshop space, library and IT access and making sure buildings are cleaned and maintained and so on all have to be priced into a research contract. Having professional support means that the academic can focus on the ideas for the proposal itself rather than getting bogged down in the finer detail.

An increasingly important role for a research department is in preparing for the Research Excellence Framework (REF) exercise. It would be unrealistic to expect academics across a university to organise a single return on behalf of the institutions – somebody needs to coordinate the information and present it in the appropriate format. This has to be done within the context of the institution's strategy for research. It might be conducted in collaboration with a research committee but is essentially undertaken by academic-related, rather than academic, staff.

Another function of the research department is to support academics in managing knowledge transfer or commercialisation of research outputs. This might mean providing guidance on starting up a small business to exploit new knowledge or products, helping to acquire patents or to protect intellectual property. Such activities are highly specialised and it makes economic sense for a university to ensure academic researchers are supported in these ways.

Enterprise

Nowadays, the research department often encompasses the university's enterprise function, although this may sit with departments responsible for corporate development. Enterprise activity, sometimes referred to as 'third stream', is more commercial than research. It refers to forms of commercial engagement, such as providing certificated or accredited Continuous Professional Development (CPD) for external organisations, conducting evaluation or feasibility studies or providing support for start-ups or small businesses. It has its origins in the Thatcherite policies of encouraging self-employment but was extended under Labour higher education policy, which aimed to encourage employers and the private sector generally, to make a contribution to the cost of HE.

Many universities now employ business development staff to work with academics in spotting opportunities for income generation and supporting them in exploitation. This might mean costing proposals, constructing tenders or submitting bids on behalf of departments, schools or faculties. They will be expected to carry out the outward-facing, networking activity which might result in building relationships, establishing collaborative partnerships or even philanthropic donations. Business development staff may be centrally located or dispersed across the institution but their work has to be coordinated to ensure it aligns with institutional strategic objectives. Indeed, some of their work may entail assessing strategic fit, developing business cases and obtaining the necessary approvals. How work of this type might be undertaken is discussed in Chapter 4.

Civic engagement

Universities also have a role to play in civil society. In a local context, they may work with schools and colleges in their immediate vicinity to raise aspirations, provide teacher training or develop new routes into their courses. Community groups might be encouraged to use university premises or attend public lectures. Links may be forged with local authorities or business organisations, such as the Chamber of Commerce.

At a regional level universities might be contributing to skills development and economic planning and may also advise on regional or even national policy. On the international stage, they could work with multi- or transnational governmental and non-governmental organisations. Figure 2.5 gives some examples of these kinds of initiatives.

The whole university is continuously occupied in civic engagement, but its importance has grown as reliance on public funding has increased. It is also closely linked with institutional identity and mission so the form of engagement will vary. Its location within the university generally appears under the umbrella of corporate development. Again, some coordination of activity to ensure alignment with strategy is important although the issue of academic autonomy often plays in. A university has more than one public, as do disciplines, and it would be short-sighted to force academic staff to look outwards through a single portal. However, institutions need to protect their reputation, which could be damaged through inappropriate external engagement or by excessive duplication of activity. It is not unknown for some external bodies to receive multiple approaches from different parts of the same institution, which can give an impression of disorganisation.

Figure 2.5: Examples of civic engagement

Campus Compact is an American coalition of university and colleges with a civic engagement focus. Each member is committed to community and civic involvement as a means of developing students' citizenship skills and meeting community partnership objectives. Student volunteering, university involvement in community development and supporting in-service learning are examples of activities. A specific example is the Pay it Forward initiative which encourages students' philanthropy in the form of fund-raising and volunteering as a means of enhancing communities.

Beacons for Public Engagement is a UK-wide initiative supported by the funding and research councils and the Wellcome Foundation. Six collaborative projects were funded for four years from 2008 with the support of the National Coordinating Centre for Public Engagement (NCCPE). Their role is to change the manner in which universities address the way they engage with the public. An excellent example of the outputs is the UK television series and associate web site Bang Goes the Theory, which aims to enhance the public understanding of science.

Management functions

If we look back at the structural hierarchy of universities (Figure 2.2), we see that there are some additional management functions which underpin all the activity of the university and are led at senior team level. These cover finance, human resources and estates. Management information is sometimes subsumed within financial management but data is now so crucial to planning that chief information officers or similar are also finding a place at the executive table.

Financial management

Organisations which handle budgets in the hundreds of millions of pounds need specialist support in managing their finances. The function of a university finance department is to manage the accounting function in order to record income and expenditure and produce annual audited accounts for public scrutiny. At a more complex level, it will manage budget setting, the distribution of resources, investment funds and borrowings. All universities are required to produce financial regulations which spell out the responsibilities of staff for following financial procedures, such as procurement of goods or services, receiving and making payments, obtaining appropriate insurances *et cetera*. Accounting processes are extensively automated and can allow direct input at departmental or sub-unit level, if desired.

As part of the financial management function, the Finance Director works with the university's executive to agree a Resource Allocation Model (RAM). Three main types of RAM are commonly in use: a) sharing, b) apportioning or c) charging for central support costs. These include such things as libraries and media services as well as management functions like finance and HR. In type a, the total income is top-sliced to support central departments and the balance allocated to Faculties or Schools who would then establish their own budgets on the basis of their income. In type b, the total income is distributed to Faculties or Schools and a cost apportioned for the central support services. In type c, total income is distributed and the Faculties or Schools then 'purchase' central services.

Depending on the RAM adopted, academics will have greater or lesser involvement in financial decision making. But in all cases central or overhead costs are a significant element of academic work and need to be taken into account in both incoming and outgoing transactions. Whilst there may be many occasions where an individual academic can be said to have 'earned' income by their own efforts, their salary and on-costs, the office in which they work and the library and IT resources they consume have to be paid for. Understanding how resources are allocated, knowing the financial regulations and being aware of costing and accounting processes will help academics in deciding whether an activity is worth undertaking in financial terms.

Management Information Systems

Snapping at the heels of the finance department for top place at the executive table, the department which manages the gathering and communication of institutional data has increased dramatically in importance in recent years. The joke goes that the less money governments allocate to universities the more they wish to micro-manage them. It is true to say, nevertheless, that the demand for performance data is growing as money becomes tighter and public accountability greater.

One of the main areas of reporting is student numbers. Funding depends on this, since UK governments determine the number of student places they are prepared to fund. These are allocated to universities, who are expected to fill them, within plus or minus 5 per cent. Funding is adjusted retrospectively according to how many students complete the stage of study they are currently enrolled for (ie submit the final piece of assessment) so the Management Information (MI) department has to make careful predictions and then keep accurate records of student progress. This information is submitted annually to Funding Councils and is also used by the Higher Education Statistics Agency (HESA) in England. The importance of accuracy cannot be overstated – the problems faced by London Metropolitan University in 2009 (a claw-back by HEFCE of funds in excess of £30m, resulting in financial problems for the university) demonstrate what can happen if mistakes are made.

In addition to public accountability, MI staff also have to calculate recruitment targets for the different parts of the university. These have to take into account all year numbers (thus progression must be predicted), desirable staff/student ratios, and the total numbers that can be coped with within building constraints – plus the likelihood of applicants meeting their offer. The institution must ensure that it is not penalised for over- or under-recruitment.

Other data will include retention, progression and achievement for academic purposes. Being able to see trends by age, gender, ethnicity, socio-economic background, prior qualifications and mode of study is surprisingly useful for course review and development. Examination boards are making increasing use of data of this type and feeding into quality enhancement processes.

The introduction of full economic costing (fEC), Transparent Approach to Costing (TRAC) and TRAC for Teaching (T) creates added responsibility for those producing data. Managing these processes requires MI to work closely with the finance and research and enterprise departments to ensure accurate costing and reporting of data.

Human Resource Management

Another joke amongst academics is that there are more administrators and managers than teachers and researchers in today's university. In fact the biggest growth area has been in the human resources (HR) department. In addition to supporting the attraction, recruitment and appointment of staff in all areas of the university, the HR department also encompasses development and training.

HE institutions in the UK currently deliver programmes to over two million students a year. Total staff numbered 372,455 in 2008, of whom 174,945 (47%) were academic and 197,515 (53%) non-academic (HESA, 2009). This is a substantial workforce which, if averaged over the number of UK HE institutions gives a figure of over 2000 in each. As there is considerable disparity in institutional size, some universities employ significantly higher numbers. Inevitably, there will be people leaving, new staff needed, sometimes the necessity to make redundancies, occasionally an employment tribunal to defend. As learning organisations, universities want their workforce to be effectively developed and rewarded, so expertise in HR management is crucial.

The most significant HR involvement in the HE workforce came with the introduction of the Framework Agreement after the Dearing report was published (see Chapter one), and the construction of role profiles. This was an attempt to create a single pay spine within institutions so that those with similar responsibilities would receive similar recognition and reward. Ideally, this single spine would operate across the sector but in reality it has to take account of local context and conditions. Thus, grading and rates of pay may vary from institution to institution. HR departments were responsible for managing the process of constructing role profiles and matching posts to them. In all universities this resulted in some down-grading as well as up-grading.

The logical next step in this process is to ensure that there is a sufficient, but not excessive, range of profiles for the strategic objectives of each unit and department in the university to be met. The introduction of workload management systems supports this approach to staffing as well as allowing TRAC and fEC to be carried out. At the same time performance management techniques, such as personal development review (PDR) or appraisal have been implemented for all university staff, as a mechanism for ensuring that strategic planning filters down to individual objective setting.

Whilst these features might seem overly mechanistic or managerialist, they can help academics to work out their own career paths, especially if they involve themselves in strategic planning at unit or department level. They are also means by which individuals can identify and access the training or development they need to support their career aspirations.

Estates and services

The staffing bill is the biggest cost for any university but a close second is the estate (ie buildings) and services, such as ICT, libraries, laboratories, catering and accommodation. Depending on the type of institution, there may be museums, galleries, theatres, horticultural centres or even farms to manage.

If a university is to be relevant to its public and attractive to staff and students, its estate needs to be regularly maintained and updated. As the focus of a university develops and changes, the stock of buildings it owns may no longer be suitable. At a simple level, ensuring disabled access may require significant renovation. Providing flexible space with wireless access for group or private study might require new buildings.

This might be beyond the influence of an individual academic, but should be considered by course teams in planning new or revised provision. There is little point in incorporating practical elements into a course if there is no-where for this to take place. Similarly, services must be adequate to support them.

Occasionally, universities will enter into partnerships with other institutions to gain access to the resources or facilities they need. For example, they might work with a car manufacturer who would give students access to specialist engineering facilities. Such relationships will bring academic staff into contact with the host organisation. This can be advantageous, for instance in seeking research funding, but can require delicate negotiation and compromise over, for instance, whether to adapt existing stock, buy or build anew, or seek out potential partnerships. Academic staff need to be engaged in the decision-making process to ensure that the ensuing facility is fit for purpose.

Services and facilities include library and information technology provision, media resources, reprographics, design and publications specialists and laboratory technical staff, as well as catering, cleaning and maintenance. The staff who manage and deliver these services are part of the 53 per cent of non-academic staff employed. All have a role in the smooth and efficient running of the university, even if they do not conduct research or teach students. Learning about the interdependences within the staff body is an important element of understanding the context and constraints within which the academic has to operate.

Conclusion

We have explored both the context of the university and some of the ways in which it might be managed and have looked at some of the functional requirements of delivering a university's objectives and how they might be met. We have tried to show why it is important for an academic to understand and be able to interact with the different centres of activity in the institution.

This chapter has, for example, shown why academics need to be aware of the limitations and potential of buildings and facilities when they plan new or revised programmes of study. They might need to work with recruitment and admissions teams to market courses to new groups of learners. Statistical evidence may be needed to inform monitoring and evaluation of courses or to reveal areas where enhancement might be necessary.

However, the context is only part of the picture for us as academics. Higher education is a knowledge industry but it is also people-focused. And the most important people are the learners. These come from home or abroad, are young or mature, and have different types of qualifications and experience. To teach effectively, the 21st century academic needs to know about the people they are teaching – the subject of the next chapter.

3

The new students

Introduction: Enter the new students

A tale of two lives

Alice attended a Russell group institution between 1971 and 1974 (when participation rates were approximately 17%) to study English Language and Literature. She went in with 'A' levels, received a full grant, had 12 hours of classes a week and went to all of them. There was something on every day and when she wasn't in class she was reading or working in the library. The course comprised lectures and seminars and although she wrote essays, the assessment was entirely based on end of year examinations. She had summer holiday jobs but did not work at all during term time. She did go out a lot, but not every night and really enjoyed her university years as a chance to have a good social life, to read a lot and to get away from home in a safe environment. The whole experience had a big impact on her life path but she never worried about the results, just enjoyed uni, and felt no pressure to look for employment afterwards.

Javed enrolled at a post-92 institution in 2006 (with participation rates at 42%) with a mix of 'A' level and vocational qualifications. He is living on loans to be repaid and is in permanent employment for 20 hours per week, balancing a social life with work and study. He undertakes a lot of assessed coursework as well as exams. Employment is a very strong driver and his focus is on career development. He lives at home, socialises in his existing peer group and is pragmatic about attendance and study – that is, he assesses the pros and cons of engagement. Going to uni is part of a life pattern and represents no major change to his further education experience.

Around the beginning of the 21st century the concept of the 'new' student emerged, usually in discussions about widening participation and generally as an epithet associated with perceived problems such students present. Some of the differences between old and new might best be exemplified by the composites described above, which reflect a distinction, made by Bernard Longden (2006), between 'going up to university' and 'going to uni'.

We cite these two extreme cases in order to make a point. There are still students of the first type, although possibly found in only some universities. But generally the student experience is now very different to the minority participation days of the 1970s but the basic offer has stayed the same: we still have structures geared towards minority participation in an era of mass participation. Martin Trow (1973) refers to an 'elite' system in which there is around 15 per cent participation; a 'mass' system (up to 40%) and 'universal' HE where more than 50 per cent participate. But in this current era of mass participation, there are different types of students. We still have an elite of 15 per cent: those who are able, by dint of socio-economic advantage, to be full-time students – the rest are effectively studying part-time but in a system which is all too often a watered down version of traditional HE provision.

It is not just attempts to widen participation that have produced 'new' students: a range of social, political and economic factors have contributed to the greater diversity in the higher education student body. This chapter examines these factors and explores the characteristics of the new students and the implications for the work of an academic.

Widening Participation – what is it really all about?
Widening Participation (WP) is a term which has achieved common currency in the education sector but has taken on different nuances as fluctuations in social, political and economic agendas have generated new imperatives. This section covers some of the history of WP in the UK.

The legacy of Dearing and Kennedy
The idea of Widening Participation in Higher Education was encouraged in the Dearing review of HE by the National Committee of Inquiry into Higher Education, which reported in 1997. However, a marker was also placed by Baroness Kennedy's concurrent report on further education, *Learning Works*. The latter was the result of work by a widening participation committee established by the Further Education Funding Council (now defunct) to advise on achieving their aim of promoting access to further education for people who did not currently participate but who could benefit from it. Kennedy's introduction to the report was somewhat critical of the further education sector becoming more business-like as it grew and losing its grasp on what it should be doing. She emphasised education as a weapon against poverty, as the route to social participation and active citizenship. She also argued that edu-

cation must be at the heart of regeneration in the UK, that it is the bedrock of social capital and that a nation's well-being is conditioned by the level of social capital in society. So for her, WP was about justice and equity as well as about economic advantage:

> Education strengthens the ties which bind people, takes the fear out of difference and encourages tolerance. (Kennedy, 1997:6)

Kennedy went on to make a swathe of recommendations for widening participation in the further education sector which have changed the way in which colleges and learning are perceived. She tied the proposals in to lifelong learning, to alternative forms and locations of delivery and new attitudes towards qualifications. She set the government a target of aspiring for all people to achieve at least a level 3 qualification.

The results of this report have had considerable effect on further education but successive changes in funding and freeing up the training market have resulted in some fragmentation. What is clear is that, never mind getting to level 3, there are still many, many young people leaving school without even a level 1 qualification. Many colleges have therefore had to radically rethink what they do. Some have responded by taking learning to the communities, setting up centres in deprived areas, giving free breakfasts to young people that get in on time in the morning, arranging for homework clubs, setting up child care schemes in libraries and such like.

As far as the value and purpose of education are concerned there is little difference between the Kennedy and Dearing reports.

The Dearing report declares:

> Higher education is fundamental to the social, economic and cultural health of the nation. It will contribute not only through the intellectual development of students and by equipping them for work, but also by adding to the world's store of knowledge and understanding, fostering culture for its own sake, and promoting the values that characterise higher education: respect for evidence; respect for individuals and their views; and the search for truth. Equally, part of its task will be to accept a duty of care for the wellbeing of our democratic civilisation, based on respect for the individual and respect by the individual for the conventions and laws which provide the basis of a civilised society. (Dearing, 1997:para 8)

Dearing's first recommendation was that the Government should have:

> a long term strategic aim of responding to increased demand for higher education, much of which we expect to be at sub-degree level; and that to this end,

the cap on full-time undergraduate places should be lifted over the next two to three years and the cap on full-time sub-degree places should be lifted immediately. (Dearing, 1997:para 6.52)

This was because the committee already saw increasing aspiration and performance among young people, and although the government had achieved the objective of a third of young people in HE by 2000 there was still a demand and, more importantly, a need for greater participation in order to increase economic advantage. However, in 2000 when the target was set for at least 50 per cent participation by 18-30 year olds by 2010, the sub-text regarding sub-degree places (foundation programmes, Foundation degrees etc) was momentarily lost, and there was a broad assumption that this meant recruiting more people to honours degree programmes.

Differential participation

The arrival of 2010 saw some considerable achievements, although the overall participation rate remained around 6 per cent below the 50 per cent target. But even though participation may have increased, it has not been at sub-degree level and there is very little differential participation, which Dearing saw us having a moral obligation to concern ourselves with. These differentials are gender, socio-economic background, locality, disability, age and ethnicity. Whilst women's participation had been increasing for many years and, in 1997, was roughly in line with their demographic representation, they were disproportionately appearing in some disciplines and not others – for instance many women studied in humanities (English, French, Sociology) but far fewer in computing, engineering or technology. Although women now outnumber men on all but post-graduate courses (the proportion stands at around 60%), they still tend to be concentrated in specific subject areas. There are considerable similarities here with expansion in France in the 1960s – many more women took up courses but tended to be concentrated in what were termed 'soft' subjects.

The participation of ethnic minority groups is similarly problematic, even though they are more than proportionally represented in HE. For example, in 1994, 8.2 per cent of the 18-20 age group from ethnic minorities were participating in HE, compared with 5.2 per cent in the wider population. This relative overrepresentation continues but it disguises some significant disparities. Considerable differences are evident when we look at specific ethnic groups, particularly Bangladeshi women and African Caribbean men. And as with women, there is greater participation in arts and humanities and significant underrepresentation in professional programmes such as teaching. Black students are also more likely to be part-time and studying for sub-degree level qualifications. To put all this into a more shocking perspective, the Campaign for Racial Equality (CRE) revealed in 2003 that for every African Caribbean male going to university in the UK there were at least two in jail (CRE, 2003).

Rates of participation among the disabled are more difficult to gauge as they rely heavily on self-declaration and there is a feeling that this group is probably under-represented. Similarly, young people who have been raised in local authority care are highly unlikely to go to university. Mature participation in HE, on the other hand, has been increasing steadily over the last 20 years and 50 per cent of new entrants are now over 21 and 30 per cent over 30. However, they tend to be concentrated in post-92 institutions and are more likely to be studying part-time than full-time.

The areas for development which now receive most focus are those of socio-economic background and locality. Even though rates of participation for lower socio-economic groups rose during the 1980s and 90s, the ratio did not. And, interestingly, those from social classes I and II are more highly represented than their share in economic activity and in the lower groups it is lower than their share. Men in socio-economic classes IV to VII are the least likely to go to university and, if they do, they tend to be in sub-degree courses.

More recently, the definition of widening participation has been broadened to include family history of HE participation. But disadvantage has been found to be far more strongly linked to the specific areas in which people actually live. In 1992, there was a 16 per cent difference in rates between highest and lowest participation neighbourhoods. What that meant then was that if the low participation areas increased to the national average 35,000 more young people would be in HE. Despite attempts by funding councils to build on Dearing's recommendations and increase participation rates, we still have very low representation by these target groups.

Research suggests several reasons for this and key amongst them is educational achievement at 18. Many young people from disadvantaged backgrounds simply do not reach the standard required to get in. This cannot be because they lack the potential. For instance, there are huge differences in progression rates to HE and in national examination achievement rates between young people in the Greater Manchester districts of Altrincham and Wythenshawe and yet they are geographically co-located. The differences are to do with employment prospects, family income, health and well-being – all of which can contribute to levels of deprivation which affect attainment. Secondly, many young people do not recognise the value of higher education

– if they don't know anyone who has gone to university, they are less likely to see the benefits. Add to this the possibility of people living in families of three generations of worklessness and it is easy to see that aspirations might be low.

So, whilst it may seem that WP has the potential to create a much more diverse student body, the actual participation of disadvantaged groups has not been as great as anticipated. This begs the question of whether the perceived difficulties of working with new students are due to widening or increasing participation. Consider the examples in Figure 3.1:

Figure 3.1: Ways of getting to university

Joti is 19 and from a Bangladeshi background. Both her parents are unemployed and she is one of six children. She is expected to contribute to childcare and housework and is not allowed to go out alone. She attended a comprehensive school and then her local Further Education college, where she studied 'A' levels in English and History and a BTec course in Childcare. She achieved the equivalent of 4 Grade As.

Penelope attends a private girls' school where she has studied 'A' levels in English, History and French. She has had additional private tuition in English and French and has achieved 3 Grade As.

Peter is the only son of a wealthy professional couple. He has a generous allowance, no need to work, and attended a local grammar school, taking the same courses as Penelope. His GCSE results were good but he is very involved with sport and his 'A' level results were 2 Cs and a D.

All three of these students are likely to get places at university but only one could be described as a WP student. Joti's WP credentials include her ethnicity, her socio-economic status and her vocational study. However, her entry qualifications are better than Peter's and, unlike Penelope, she achieved them without the benefit of additional tutorial support. Can we tell, therefore, which student is likely to need additional support and what kind of support that might be? Or should we take on board that we will inevitably have diversity in our student body and that WP is not the only factor influencing its make-up?

If it isn't WP making a difference, then what is it?

There is an old saying that the only constant in life is change. Change occurs all around us and is so constant that, just like the earth spinning on its axis, we only seem to notice social change has occurred when we can stop and

Figure 3.2: A comparison of experiences

	Dorothy – 1930s	Sarah – 1950s	Hannah – 1980s
Employment	Worked as a nurse before marriage	Office work, continued part-time after marriage and then full-time when children self sufficient	Full-time career as voluntary sector researcher
Qualifications	School Certificate	GCE 'O' and 'A' level	GCSE, Curriculum 2000, BA,MA
Learned to drive	Mid 30s	Mid 20s	17
First flight	70	34	3
First use of computer	70	19	2
First mobile phone	75	40	12
Preferred cuisine	British	European	International

take stock. To illustrate this, Figure 3.2 shows some of the experiences of three generations of women in one family

These are certainly observable and reportable characteristics but there are other, more esoteric features which might show the passage of time. Generational theory is one such approach, which although justifiably contested, does provide a lens through which differences over time might be observed.

Generational theory and the student body

The origins of generational theory lie in the work of Mannheim (1952). More influential analysis has been conducted by Strauss and Howe (1991), later picked up by other writers with an interest in students, such as Coomes and DeBard (2004) and Paul Redmond (2007). Strauss and Howe argue that generations identified by bounded time periods are significantly shaped by historical events or characteristics. Each generation will then go on to shape the next cycle of events which in turn shape the generation living through them. Without doubt, any theory which attempts to categorise people according to a period within which they were born is as open to accusations of pseudo-science as astrology. Numerous questions are invited relating to geography, social class, ethnicity and so on and how these might undermine the notion of distinct, identifiable generational groups. However, there are some commonly observable attributes which might be useful, indeed more useful than 'widening participation', in explaining increasing diversity among HE students.

Strauss and Howe identified three generations: 'the silents', 'the baby boomers' and the 'generation Xers'. Since then generation Y, or 'the millennial', has been added to the list (Strauss and Howe, 1991). Whilst some features might be contestable from our own experiences, there are significantly recognisable features which give some credence to this way of seeing students. Figure 3.3 below highlights some of the features which might be observable in a university environment, including staff and students, determined by their birth years. These have been culled from a variety of sources.

Figure 3.3: Generational experiences

Silents (1925-1942)	Baby Boomers (1943-1960)	Generation X (1961-1981)	Generation Y (1982-2002)
World War II, Cold War	Vietnam War, Civil rights movements	Cold War, Fall of Berlin Wall, Gulf War	Iraqi war, War on terror
Wall street crash, war time austerity	Post-war growth, optimism	Growth of service economy, knowledge industries	Economic uncertainty, no jobs-for-life
Work ethic	Social relationships	Work as means to an end	Career focus – fun at work
Respect for hierarchical authority	Want to be involved in decision-making	Value independence in decisions affecting self	Want direct say in how work is done. Little faith in government
Respect for social authority, value of roles, knowing ones place in society	'Me' generation, self-fulfilment, social status important	Success = survival, enjoyment, independence, consumption	Strong self-belief, want socially responsible employers, pessimistic about the future
Digital Virgins	Digital novices	Digital immigrants	Digital natives

Generation Y as students

Whilst it is likely for there to be a mixture of generations in any one setting, the majority of the student population is likely to be made up of generation Y. Paul Redmond (2008a) has highlighted additional features and some of the rules which seem to apply. In terms of aspiration, they seek change, challenge and choice; a sense of purpose and meaning; access to mentors rather than bosses and they prefer open, honest social networks. For the fortunate amongst them, computers are furniture and their parents are their personal equivalent of the American Strategic Defence Initiative, providing a protective shield, fighting their battles for them and bailing them out of difficulties, especially financial ones.

These last two factors bear closer scrutiny. Although the origins of the intenet can be traced back to the 1960s, universities did not make much use of computers for communication until the 1980s and they did not appear in homes until the 1990s. Google was founded in 1998 so even for Generation Y, it is a relatively new phenomenon. Similarly, mobile phones can be traced back to the 1950s but useable versions (ie less than the weight of a wall-brick) did not come on to the market until the 1990s and 3G phones of the type which are common today were first introduced commercially in 2001.

Today's very young children can take photos with mobile phones, upload them to computers and email them to their family. At the same time, they are mocking previous generations for texting words in full. A recent undergraduate of our acquaintance had the unnerving ability to text on two mobile phones at once, one in each hand! Although many of us are now accustomed to buy books or groceries, download music, do our banking and book holidays or train journeys on-line, for Generation Y it is much more a way of life. Why visit the library for a book, when you can just Google for a fast response? Why ring friends individually when you can catch up and have multiple conversations though Facebook?

All this activity though, is conducted for many, in a protected environment. Redmond (2008b) picks up on the trend for parents to be heavily involved in their children's lives, especially when it comes to university. In part, he says, this could be a response to the marketisation of higher education – parents are contributing much more to the cost and therefore want a say in what they get for their money. They are also more concerned about their child's wellbeing and safety and have a tendency to hover like helicopters around their offspring. Redmond identifies five types: the agents who operate as a personal Max Clifford, the bankers who are resigned to making a loss, the white knights who fly in to the rescue when needed, the bodyguards who take flak on their child's behalf and the black hawks who will go to any lengths to support their child's advancement. According to Furedi (2003), this 'infantilisation' creates 'kidults' or 'adultescents' who are physically mature but treated as, and behave like, children.

The cost of higher education and the need for many young people to combine work and study has led to a big increase in the numbers of young people who stay at home, rather than go away to university. University UK's *Sixth Patterns* report (Ramsden, 2006) showed that between 1995/6 and 2004/5 the numbers of students living at home with their parents increased from 12 per cent to 20 per cent, and the numbers living in halls of residence fell over the same period from 35 per cent to 27 per cent. But even those who have moved out of the family home are still within constant technological reach.

General features of the behaviour of generation Y have been summarised by Paul Redmond (2008a), and are listed in Figure 3.4, below.

Some of these, especially the issue of attendance, can prove challenging for boomers and Xers but need not be deal-breakers. If we use Generation Y features to think about implications for learning and teaching, it might mean we have to do some things differently, but it doesn't make it impossible. Figure 3.5 opposite contains some suggestions for dealing with the rules, one for adapting academic practice, the other for improving alignment between practice and behaviour.

Figure 3.4: behaviour of generation Y

For generation Y, attendance is always optional.

They are passionate about new challenges, responsibilities and success.

A career means a cause to believe in.

They are very competitive and entrepreneurial.

Work/life balance is more than just a buzz word – it means flexi- and part-time working, gap years and home working

They want feedback and they want it now.

They are brand literate.

Equality, transparency and fairness are paramount.

They respond best to coaches rather than bosses.

They will challenge frequently and they will quit. (Redmond, 2008a)

Figure 3.5: impact of generation Y on practice

The 'Rule'	Adapting practice	Changing practice
Attendance is optional	Make it worthwhile to turn up	Make greater use of technology
New challenges, responsibilities, success.	Find a way to give ownership, celebrate success	Involve students in design of learning
A career means a cause	Focus materials on social responsibility	Build career planning into curriculum
Competitive and entrepreneurial	Be innovative in assessment	Use more Approved Prior Experiential Learning (APEL)
Importance of work life balance	Make use of informal learning contexts	Provide flexible routes through programmes
Feedback now	Make feedback immediate and detailed	Consider replacing grades with learning outcome commentaries
Equality, transparency and fairness are paramount	Ensure materials and delivery are completely inclusive	Challenge assumptions
Coaches not bosses	Tutorial support rather than didactic delivery	Integrate buddy systems, mentoring and peer support
Challenging and prepared to quit	Always stay one step ahead and make sure everything counts	Support challenge and set parameters for student influence on curriculum and delivery

'Net Genners' – the influence of technology

In our proposition that social change may affect student characteristics, we referred to the difference between digital immigrants and digital natives. Net genners is another term used to describe those born into a technical world very different to that of twenty or thirty years ago. As we argued, telephones, radio and television have been around for almost the entire life-span of the current population of the UK, although access has been more or less dependent on socio-economic status. However, for those born in the last twenty years, the internet and mobile devices have always been there.

The most remarkable element of this aspect of change is the pace at which it has occurred. At the time of writing, there are over 500 million active Facebook users, 65 million of them accessing from mobile devices, whilst in China, Qzone is said to have already outstripped these figures. Numbers of Twitter users can only be guessed at but is already in the hundreds of millions. The preferred forms of interaction amongst most net genners are SMS messaging and social networking sites such as Facebook, or Myspace. The most widely used search engine is Google, and Wikipedia now has more than 3 million entries, many of which are allegedly as accurate as the Encyclopaedia Britannica. Mobile learning, through iTunesU, is also growing rapidly, with 600 universities making material available for their students.

What does this mean for those of us working with students? Do they prefer to access their learning through the same channels as their social interaction? Or is it too early to say? Research undertaken at the Open University would suggest that there is as much diversity in the take-up of technology as there is currently in the student body (Jones *et al*, 2010). Preliminary findings indicate that most people are happy to work in whatever way the course is delivered. Some would still prefer paper-based texts and face to face interaction, whilst others would opt for a purely on-line experience. But there does seem to be some resistance to the idea of using social-networking channels for study purposes. Some universities have begun to experiment with Second Life environments, especially as a means of creating a safe space for practicing learning, but these are not yet widespread. The use of wikis (web pages which can be edited collaboratively by groups of people) is also becoming common.

Technological change of this nature raises issues for university academics. One concerns the environment and facilities. Learning spaces need to be flexible as different approaches to information provision are accommodated. Wireless internet connection is becoming increasingly common in university buildings and environs, and collaborative work spaces are more frequently provided. Academic staff need to adjust to working in such a context and be sufficiently familiar with the technological infrastructure to support students.

The second issue concerns the relationship between the student and tutor – technology allows for an immediacy which can affect the dynamic. When a student emails a tutor or posts a comment on a discussion site their expectation of an immediate and individual response is much higher than if they were attending a tutorial with a dozen other students or submitting a piece of written work for comment. Managing such expectations is essential if a 24 hour working day is to be avoided. A related issue concerns the possible skills disparity between digital native students and digital immigrant tutors. Keeping one step ahead is time consuming and demanding.

Also an issue is the extent to which technology can be used in gaining unfair advantage or invite academic misconduct. Facilities such as Turnitin or Copy-catch might recognise material which is copied from electronic sources, but they are less effective in identifying an essay which has been purchased from one of the many electronic providers now advertising on the internet. We discuss these issues in chapter five.

Globalisation and internationalisation

Another, more recent phenomenon in universities all over the world is the increasing number of overseas or international students. This is partly a result of globalisation, but is also due to the increasing marketisation of higher education. How has this happened and what does it mean for an academic?

According to Malcolm Waters, globalisation is 'a social process in which the constraints of geography on social and cultural arrangements recede and in which people become increasingly aware that they are receding' (Waters, 1995:3). This definition, however, neglects a key controversial element of globalism – that it tends to move from West to East and can be seen as an extension of colonialism or another form of imperialism. This is particularly true in higher education. Cohen and Kennedy (2000) explicitly link the emergence of a world society to specific factors: modernity in Western Europe, the growth of powerful and wealthy nation states, cultural and scientific enlightenment, the growth of rationality, the extension of capitalism, and attempts to 'civilise' the world through colonisation and the subjection of other races and cultures.

Economic and political power are, therefore, particularly important to trends in globalisation. For example, with the emergence of America as a dominant economic and political power during the 20th century the emphasis of globalisation was seen to shift to Americanisation, with the rise of mass consumption and the spread of English as an international language. As Thomas Friedman put it:

> Globalisation has a distinctly American face: It wears Mickey Mouse ears, it eats Big Macs, it drinks Coke or Pepsi and does its computing on an IBM or Apple laptop, using Windows 98, with an Intel Pentium processor and a network link from Cisco systems. (Friedman, 2000:309)

This is largely a result of the major trans-national corporations having their origins in the US.

Whilst there have been many (disputed) interpretations of globalisation, the key elements affecting the higher education sector are the compression of space and time brought about by developments in transport, and communications technology. McLuhan (1964) refers to the 'new world of the global village' (p93) in which 'implosion' (p185) is brought about by faster transport and speedier communications, allowing us all to experience simultaneously events which happen anywhere in the world. Giddens maintains that 'Globalisation can thus be defined as the intensification of worldwide social relations which link distant localities in such a way that local happenings are shaped by events occurring many miles away and vice versa' (Giddens, 1990: 64). This has important implications for teaching in HE.

Globalisation and higher education

In the world of HE, enhanced mobility and the advent of mobile internet connection mean that students can more easily travel to other parts of the world to study, as might researchers or teaching staff. At the same time, distance learning and international collaboration imply the possibility that the benefits of universities and their outputs might be more equitably spread across the world. To put it another way, it could mean that we are teaching more people from other parts of the world, with academic and student co-located either in the student's home country or the academic's, or with each home-based but connected by technology of one form or another.

By far the commonest experience for the academic in the UK is to be teaching international students alongside home students. Some may come from European countries and be on exchange schemes, others from the Far East can be under-graduate or post-graduate students. The problems they face are fairly standard – they are to do with language, culture and approaches to learning. Courses in UK universities are generally taught through the medium of English language. It is usually a requirement for home students to have a minimum proficiency in English, demonstrated through GCSE qualifications or similar. For overseas students entry requirements usually include a level score in a language assessment test. For most universities, the International English Language Testing System (IELTS) is the qualification of choice, although some also accept the Test of English as a Foreign Language (TOEFL). These tests give the candidate a score which indicates their proficiency. Typically, universities will ask for a score of around 6 or 6.5 for under-graduate entry and higher for post-graduate courses. The more research-intensive universities, which have higher entry requirements generally, may ask for even higher IELTS scores.

But scoring at a benchmark level for entry is not the same as using a language to live and study in another country. Many international students find the transition very difficult and often have to learn additional languages – those which are used in universities to describe practice and processes and those which include regional idiosyncrasies or are informed by dialect. Culture clash is also possible – one of the most frequently cited aspects of UK university life which many international students find difficult to deal with is the way social life tends to revolve around drinking alcohol.

The curriculum itself can create barriers for international students, particularly if it uses only localised examples and illustrations. Cultural sensitivities around gender, sexuality, death or disease, for instance, may have to be carefully considered, even though they may not always be accommodated. Delivery might also be problematic, especially if students have become used to didactic approaches in which they are recipients of linear knowledge transfer rather than co-creators of understanding. In some parts of the world, the belief that the tutor or lecturer is the expert and always right can lead to ideas being repeated parrot – fashion in assessments. What appears to the student to be a way of showing respect may be taken by the UK academic as plagiarism.

Diversity and Equality Legislation

As we have seen in this chapter, increasing – rather than widening – access, social, economic and technological change and globalisation have made significant contributions to the diversity of the student body. But it is not just change in the cohorts we have to consider. There is also legislation which governs our behaviour and patterns the expectations of both staff and students.

Diversity is mostly seen as incorporating the main equality strands of age, gender, ethnicity, disability, religion and sexuality. Diversity is sometimes visible, sometimes not. Other categories into which members of a university community might fall which could not be said to be visible but which contribute to the diversity of the membership are: social class, the person's level of education or skills, their health and employment, where they live, their hobbies and interests and their marital or family status. Such characteristics render us different from each other. Tolerance for these differences is an essential part of our moral and ethical position but prejudice and discrimination do exist. The Equalities Act 2010 is the latest legislation in pursuit of inclusivity and social justice.

Sexual discrimination and race relations bills were first passed in the 1970s. These have since been revised and all the equality strands are now covered in law. The Race Relations (Amendment) Act 2000 which came into force in 2002 calls for a positive duty to promote racial equality rather than just providing protection against discrimination.

In the HE sector, the Equality Challenge Unit (ECU) was established in 2001 to promote equality for staff, and its brief was extended in 2006 to include equality and diversity issues for students. The ECU defines equal opportunities, or equality of opportunity, as ensuring that everyone is entitled to freedom from discrimination. This encompasses equality of treatment.

Disability

Until 1995, disabled people in the Uk had no protection from discrimination in accessing education, work, services or transport. The Disability Discrimination Act, introduced that year, made major differences but it was the Amendment to the act in 2005 which really promoted positive action and laid an anticipatory duty on organisations, including universities. In addition to ensuring that the institution meets the needs of all its students, it must now also ensure that it is not potentially discriminating through having inaccessible buildings or services. At the very least the university must be able to show that they can make any reasonable adjustments required. Disability, for the purpose of the Act, refers to any physical or mental impairment which has a long term, substantial adverse effect on a person's ability to carry out normal day to day activities. In the university context this would include people with learning difficulties such as dyslexia or dyspraxia.

For university staff working with disabled students, then, there are considerations which go well beyond accessible buildings. Is travel between classrooms feasible within the timetable? Do the rooms have space for wheelchair users, hearing loops fitted and adequate lighting? Personal evacuation plans for disabled students also need to be in place, in case of emergency. Personal learning plans have to be created and the information disseminated to relevant people, especially those who are actually teaching the student. These might include requirements for large print handouts, providing lecture notes in advance, using specific colours of paper or ensuring that computer interfaces meet accessibility standards. Special arrangements for assessment might be necessary, such as arranging separate rooms, additional time or even providing an amanuensis. A tutor might also be working with a student who has a support worker or note-taker with them in class. This can be challenging to manage as it may impact on classroom dynamics.

The duty of care the university has for disabled students extends to any place-ment or exchange which takes place as part of the course of study. This can be difficult to accommodate, particularly if the student is travelling to another country where legislation is less supportive.

Age

In 2006, UK equalities legislation was expanded with the addition of the Em-ployment Equality (Age) Regulations to the statute book for England, Wales and Scotland. The purpose of the legislation is to protect people from age dis-crimination in employment, training and adult education. Effectively, nobody may be treated less favourably than anyone else in the context of recruitment, promotion, terms and conditions, redundancy and dismissal for reasons of their age. Whilst the official retirement age stays at 65, employees may apply to continue working and age restrictions on statutory redundancy, unfair dis-missal and statutory sick pay have been removed.

The regulations make direct and indirect discrimination, harassment and victimisation on grounds of age unlawful. However, voluntary work is not covered, nor is the provision of goods and services – it is still lawful for in-surers or health providers to discriminate on grounds of age. Thus, despite protection in the areas of employment and education and training, there is still scope for ageism in our society.

Discrimination on the grounds of age is not a major issue for universities. There is no limit on the age at which one can study, although access to fund-ing may be difficult for older learners and recruiting young students (under 18) would require all staff to undergo Criminal Records Bureau checks. Academics who have worked with mature students often find it a positive ex-perience, as they tend to bring a wealth of life experience alongside high levels of commitment and engagement and considerable drive and ambition. It has been said that if you give a young student a mark in the 60s they will be satisfied, but give a mature student a mark in the 80s and they will want to know what they have done wrong!

Mature students may have been out of education for a long time and might need to acquire appropriate study skills. It can be difficult to manage classes with a mix of young and mature students. The youngsters can feel less free to express themselves confidently, whilst the mature students may resent the lack of preparation or engagement by the younger students. The tutor or lecturer has to maximise everyone's opportunity for contributing and be care-ful not to use illustrations which might be generation- or age-specific.

Finally, older students may have caring or other domestic responsibilities which restrict their ability to engage at the expected level. This does not mean they cannot succeed but they may need to be granted some leeway or given additional support.

Ethnicity

The Race Relations (Amendment) Act 2000 puts a duty on universities to consider the ways in which they will work towards, monitor and assess race equality, the responsibilities of staff and the equality impact any policy or practice will have. Probably the area to receive most attention is monitoring statistical data associated with recruitment, retention, progression and outcome. We saw that although ethnic minority students are over-represented in universities relative to their proportion in the population as a whole, they are concentrated in particular disciplines and new universities, studying vocational courses, with law and health-related courses the most popular. In some subject areas, especially art and design related subjects, including performing arts, they are woefully absent.

Data has shown that ethnic minority student achievement levels in terms of degree classification tend to be lower than for their white peers. A Higher Education Academy programme conducted in 2009 suggests that pedagogic approaches, curriculum content and assessment practices are at the root of this. It has been suggested that such students need to be taught the rules of the game. But perhaps institutions need to review the rules of engagement!

Gender

In the days of minority participation there was a clear gender differential in universities. This is hardly surprising in a sector which completely excluded women for most of its 800 year history. However, since the 1960s, there has been a gradual trend for more women to take up university places. Women, too, tend to be concentrated in certain disciplines, often in so-called softer subjects such as the humanities, social sciences or psychology. So great is the gender shift, however, that there is now talk of a reverse gender gap, with lack of young white male participation now seen as problematic.

Women are beginning to overtake men in terms of good degree classifications but more firsts still go to men. This is reflected in post-graduate participation rates but may change as masters programmes are seen as a way of achieving further differentiation in the job market and more women move through the system. Whilst this might suggest the feminisation of universities, most vice-chancellor and senior manager positions are still held by men.

Paid work and study: the need to live and learn

Another shift in universities relates to mode of study. Part-time study for a degree is becoming more common – the success of the Open University and Birkbeck College are testament to this. However, in the conventional sector it is fair to say that part-timers are not well supported. More often than not part-time provision merely entails allowing access to full-time courses over a longer period. For those in full-time work, courses are impossible to access without the cooperation of their employers. Even when part-time study comprises evening or weekend provision, students may find themselves in half lit buildings on semi-deserted campuses without access to library or IT resources, cafeterias or student support services. So the part-time student often has a very unwelcoming experience at university, having to drink coffee from a machine in an unlit cafeteria or classroom and being followed round the building by house staff with bunches of keys, chasing them out. All but the central computer drop-ins close early so there is nowhere for them to print out their coursework without trekking across the campus.

In institutions at the other end of the spectrum, classes for full-time students are shoed in between 9am and 4pm, with most people going for a 10am start because 'students won't turn up for 9am' and a last class at 3pm 'because they never want to stay late'. But the fact is that most students today undertake paid work for at least part of their time at university. Funding arrangements are such that a combination of loan and overdraft may just cover the cost of accommodation during term time, so without parental or partner support, most students need to work if they want to eat.

For students with dependents, the need to generate additional income while studying is often crucial and they may be working night shifts, at weekends and full- or part-days in the week. Attendance at classes and time for self-study or preparation might therefore be sacrificed in the interest of subsistence.

A related trend can be seen in the number of students, especially young participants, who are opting to stay in the family home rather than moving away to study. For example, this might be a cultural restriction for women from Asian heritage communities but for many people it is an economic necessity – their families cannot afford to subsidise their study in any other way. Paul Redmond (2007) memorably referred to the concept of 'wash and go' students, in a phrase capturing the cultural shift in the student population of many universities. Engagement with university life is of a different order when students are coming in purely to attend classes and returning home for their jobs and social lives.

The change in the university offer and its delivery is also contributing to a change in the nature of the student body. The addition of foundation degrees, delivered through workplace or in partnership with local further education colleges or private work-based learning providers also contributes to the current mix of students we work with in higher education.

Summary

This chapter challenges the view that the diversity of the student body and the nature of the new student are inevitable consequences of the widening participation agenda and shows that these are rather the result of social, political and economic change, *increases* in participation rates generally and changes in government policy. It also highlights the full range of diversity that academics working in higher education can expect.

According to HESA, in 2008/9 there were 2,396,055 HE enrolments in the UK. Of these, 1,540,035 were full-time (64%) and 10 per cent (251,310) were from outside the EU. According to the Higher Education Policy Institute (Bekhradnia, 2007), 67 per cent of full-time higher education first degree entrants are under 21, and 85 per cent are under 30.

Analysis of HESA, HEPI and HEFCE data suggest that currently approximately 60 per cent of UK undergraduates are women and they outnumber men on all but post-graduate research programmes. In the 1970s women made up approximately 30 per cent of the cohort, while in the 1960s and in 1986 this figure stood at 20 per cent and 46 per cent respectively. Registration on part-time courses has shown a slight rise, whilst full-time enrolments continue to rise. The age of part-time undergraduates, meanwhile, has stayed fairly static: most are over the age of 30.

In 2007/8 ethnic minority students made up 34 per cent of new enrolments. Seven per cent of students disclosed a disability, of which 23 per cent were specific learning difficulties (such as dyslexia). HEFCE also show that of the 37,460 people who completed apprenticeships in 2002/3, 8 per cent progressed onto higher education courses (HEFCE, 2009).

Our student body is, indeed, diverse and we may want to speak of 'new' students. What we must avoid is treating this newness in a pejorative way. The diversity we now experience in our student cohorts is the result of all kinds of change: social, political, economic and technological. As academics and HE practitioners, we are subject to the same kinds of influences but have not heard, as yet, of any accusation that academics themselves are less able, less well-prepared or less engaged with what they do.

Part Two
Working in higher education in the 21st century

4

The basic academic role

Introduction

A Day in the Life....

Sally gets into work at about 9am. She spends half an hour checking her emails before her first meeting, a Faculty Employability working group on which she is departmental representative. The group reviews some survey data collected from employers and decides on follow-up actions. At 10.45 Sally excuses herself and goes to the seminar room for her 11am tutorial. One of the students stays behind afterwards to ask for some help, and after talking to him and then detouring to pick up a sandwich at the coffee shop, Sally is back at her desk by 12.30. She reviews her notes for her 2pm lecture and checks that she has all her handouts. An email alert for a new journal issue occupies her until it's time to leave. Her lecture is followed by a two hour laboratory class, and at 5pm she goes back to her office and spends another half an hour dealing with email before picking up a few notes to read on the train, and setting off for home.

Meanwhile, Ye has spent the morning in meetings and the rest of the day in writing grant applications, Nasreen had a precious research day split between the library and an SPSS data analysis, while Alan worked through a pile of marking.

Looking at the role profile for a new lecturer in UK Higher Education, one might be forgiven for wondering how Universities manage to recruit anybody, given the range of requirements that are listed. The post of lecturer is incredibly varied: it includes lecturing, tutoring, marking, researching, providing pastoral support to students and doing academic administration: the sheer diversity can be one of its joys. The downside to this variety is the expectation for an academic to be a Jack of many trades, although not straight away.

This chapter is designed to support immediate immersion into the academic role and concentrates on the aspects of the role which need to be mastered quickly. An academic new in role is most likely to be teaching on courses designed by somebody else, so we focus on lecturing, tutoring and marking, followed by researching, student support and administration.

Lecturing

'If all the students asleep in lectures were laid end to end ... they'd all be a lot more comfortable' (anon).

It's a Friday afternoon, about halfway through the autumn term. It's already getting dark outside, and it seems to have been raining for days. The lecture theatre, which seats about 200, has around 40 students sitting in it, spread out around the room, with damp coats on the seats next to them. Dr Meanwell is hitting her stride in her lecture on Medieval Poetry. The students are taking lots of notes and they seem to be listening attentively.

Across the corridor, she can occasionally hear Professor Popular, who must be lecturing in the theatre opposite. Every now and then there are bursts of laughter, and sometimes she can hear a student's voice. She wonders briefly what's happening in there, but she knows that Professor Popular is a bit of a performer – he often cracks jokes in departmental meetings – and it's easy to make jokes out of 19th century literature, anyway. She carries on with her notes – there's a lot to get through.

At the end of the hour she brings the lecture neatly to a close, and her students file out quietly and bump into the lively crowd coming out of the lecture theatre opposite. There seems to have been a full house in the other session, and quite a few of them are talking enthusiastically about a dilemma which Professor Popular has posed at the end of the session. Dr Meanwell feels a bit downcast: she's sure the students who came to her lecture got a lot out of it, but half the class was missing, and she didn't get much feedback from the ones who were there. Yet she'd spent ages preparing, and she knows that she covered all the ground they will need for the exam. Surely Professor Popular couldn't have got through as much, with all the interruptions, and the jokes?

The Oxford Pocket English dictionary says that a lecture is a 'talk giving specified information to a class' (Hawker and Elliot, 2005). We know that lecturing began in medieval Universities when no copies of books were available: the lecturer would read out the original version of the book for the students to copy down. Our notion of what a lecture is has changed since the Middle Ages – lecturers usually read from their own notes rather than those of a source, and they often do things other than reading, using a variety of ways of communicating information and ideas to a group. A lecturer today is: *a member of academic staff teaching a large group of students* and the lecture still appears on the timetables of most students and most members of academic staff.

There are a few born lecturers, but most of us have to learn how to do it and develop the skills through practice. We know from our own experiences of being on the receiving end that there is a variety of practice and that some approaches work better than others. It can be difficult to maintain attention on a speaker for a full hour and it's not always easy to take good notes. There have been studies showing that this is a common experience (eg Bligh, 2000) and that it is difficult for the brain to process information consistently over the length of a typical lecture. There are a couple of good books (Brown and Race, 2002; Race and Pickford, 2007) which cover these skills in detail, but for the purposes of this chapter we provide brief guidance on planning and delivering lectures.

Planning

The first challenge is to work out what each lecture is intended to achieve. The notion of personal interaction is a good place to start thinking about the individual sessions. What is it that we offer that the textbook cannot? How will getting learning material in lectures differ from getting the content from a book? What will be the Unique Selling Point of each individual lecture? What will happen in each lecture to make it unmissable for students? How will each session relate to the assessment for the module and add to the essential skills students need to develop? Diana Laurillard (2002) once said that we didn't give out degrees for spending three years in the library; lecturers and the way they present the material are important to the process of a new student becoming the person who is awarded a degree: we change the way people think about the subject as well as providing information about subject content. A good starting point, then, is to make a list of what it is that the students should able to do by the end of each session – Figure 4.1 overleaf provides some prompts to start this process.

Next we can think about what students need to be told in order to meet these objectives. As well as the syllabus, it is important to think about all the following

- what students could do before they came to the lecture
- what students will be doing before the next session
- what students will be doing in the next session
- how this session relates to the assessment for the module

Figure 4.1 Some examples of primary objectives of a lecture – what should students be able to do on leaving a lecture?

Produce a précis of an article, a point of view or a technique?

Use primary sources more effectively?

Argue a case?

Compare and contrast different approaches?

Know where to find definitive primary sources?

Be familiar with an important element of the canon of the subject?

Know how to perform a particular calculation?

Be confident about key health and safety issues?

Be able to prioritise topics that are important?

Have observed a worked example?

Each module should be split up into neat sections, and each lecture planned around delivering just one section of content. But planning around *process* as well as *content* can suggest more activities that students can do in lectures to reinforce the skills they should develop, and make effective links between sections of the course.

Delivery
Introduction
How might a lecture be introduced as an event? If visual presentation aids such as MS Powerpoint™ are being used then having a cartoon, photograph or other image on the screen as people come in and get settled can attract their attention. It could be:

- something simple which illustrates directly the topic
- something which is somewhat tenuously linked to the topic, to get them thinking about what the relevance to the lecture might be
- something amusing about the topic
- something which illustrates current affairs related to the topic

Occasionally, placing an unusual object on the desk which has a link to the lecture, or playing music (subject to the university having a performing rights licence) can be thought-provoking.

Once everyone is settled, a good, clear introduction is essential to signal that it's time to concentrate. This should include a short overview of what's coming up, how it relates to what they've done already and to the assessment. It is usually good practice to make some reference to the intended learning outcomes for the session. Any issues picked up from previous weeks could also be mentioned.

Interactions

Sustaining attention on a speaker can be difficult, however lively and engaging they may be. It's better to break up the lecture with one or two opportunities for doing something other than listening, for example:

- ask students to work in pairs to summarise the lecture so far and then to discuss their summary with the pair sitting behind or in front of them

- ask specific questions, such as 'why do you think [the topic I've just covered] is important?'

- suggest that each pair try to think of a quick test question on the material that has just been covered for the pair sitting behind/in front of them and see if the other pair can answer correctly

- as students are coming in, give out a double-sided sheet with a different image on each side, a red tomato and a green pepper, or something which represents opposites in the subject area. The different sheets must be easily visible at a distance, so use contrasting colours. At various points in the lecture, ask a question which can be answered with yes or no, and request students to vote using their sheets. It may be a bit of a gimmick, and not something to use every time, but it will help the audience to think about a topic, and to remember it. Commercial versions of this device, such as a cube with six different coloured sides (Bostock *et al*, 2006), are available, or many institutions have electronic audience response systems (Banks, 2006) which can be borrowed for lectures.

When asking for a few sample responses after an activity, don't just make a general request – few students will feel comfortable replying, and it will usually be the same ones who do. But don't pick on one individual either. Ask 'someone from the top right' or 'one of that lively group in the left hand corner' to answer. Go over to that area of the room if necessary, especially if people are having difficulty in settling down again. Always praise the participation itself, even if the answer is wrong – 'thanks for having a go at that, you might need to think a bit more about...'

When breaking for an activity, always make clear:

- what the purpose of the activity is and how it relates to the rest of the lecture
- what signal will be used to end the activity (eg clapping hands, flashing the lights, bell, alarm clock, playing the trumpet).
- *Exactly* what they are being asked to do – check this with a friend or colleague beforehand so there's no ambiguity

If it seems difficult to get participation going, don't despair. The students need to get used to it too. Reiterate the relevance to the learning outcomes of the unit, and refer to research showing that this kind of participation helps with learning (Race and Pickford, 2007).

Distractions

Think about the various distractions which might disturb delivery of the lecture, such as late arrivals, early departures, mobile phone use or chatting, before they happen. These kinds of things will happen in lectures, and in some cases there may be good reasons for them: for instance, possible valid reasons for each of those examples might be poor timetabling elsewhere, caring responsibilities, sick relatives or non-native English speakers needing a translation.

Disruption should not be ignored. Students will find it distracting. But your response must be calm. Do not make a public example of the individual – that may make them think twice about attending lectures. Check out the reasons for their behaviour with the student privately if their disruptions are persistent, and see if there is a solution. Turning up late but discreetly is better than not coming at all.

What you expect of the audience should be made clear at the start. Remind students to switch off mobile phones at the beginning of each lecture and tell them as often as necessary that chatting, phoning and texting are unacceptable in lectures. Ask students who do arrive on time to move around before the start, leaving spaces near the exits and aisles, so latecomers can sit down without creating disturbance.

Some lecturers resort to promising to answer a phone themselves if it rings in class, or giving the rest of the lecture standing next to the offender, but this kind of thing should not be attempted unless you definitely have confidence to carry it through.

Ending the lecture

The old maxim is 'First I tell them what I'm going to tell them, then I tell them, then I tell them what I've told them'. This still works. As well as a good introduction, a session needs a good ending: a short recap of the intended outcomes and a reminder of what they are expected to do following the lecture.

The 'one minute paper' (Stead, 2005) is a good technique to use to evaluate the session or to get an idea of what students may have struggled with during the lecture. Students spend one minute trying one of the following instructions:

- Write down what you consider to have been the main purpose of this session
- Write down a question you would now like to ask me OR a comment you would like to make about the session
- Write down at what point in the lecture you got lost ('the Muddiest Point')
- Complete a sentence such as 'Today I had difficulty with...' or 'the best part of the session was...' or 'I'm going to follow up the session by....'
- Write down something you didn't understand at all
- Answer a simple question (if possible) on the subject matter
- Draw the relationship between topics covered at different points in the lecture.

Questions can be varied from week to week to get an overall picture of what's going on with the students; they will get bored if they are asked to do the same thing every week.

Even with a very large group, it doesn't take long to collect up and skim through these papers, and it gives quick and valuable feedback on what students got out of the session. It also gives shy students a chance to contribute or give feedback if they don't feel confident enough to speak out in a lecture. Any commonly expressed problems can be addressed in the following week's lecture, or via electronic communication. Showing students that they are being listened to encourages them to raise any difficulties in the future.

Follow-up

Lectures should not be seen as isolated incidents. Consideration needs to be given to how they fit in with other things that students are doing in the unit or elsewhere on their course and how what is covered in the lecture relates to the module assessment. If a clear idea of these relationships is communicated to students systematically, they will be better able to make connections themselves and to fix the lecture content in its proper context. At the beginning of each session, they should be reminded of what happened last time, and how today's material will be developed in future sessions. At the end, review what has been covered and explain how it links into any tasks being set before the next session, as well as what will happen in the next session. Make the notes available electronically, and if possible, set some follow-up work such as reading, problem-solving or note-writing.

Evaluation

The performance element of lecturing means that we dwell more on unsuccessful lectures than on other activities which may have been unsuccessful, such as meetings – but we have to accept that some lectures work better than others. A quick analysis of what went well, what could have been better and what needs to be worked on – a personal one minute paper – will provide a checklist for future lecture preparation and presentation.

Tutoring

It's 9 o'clock on Tuesday morning. Dr Hopeful finishes rearranging the chairs in the seminar room as the first students come in and take off their coats, organise their pads, and chat quietly to each other. At five past, about half the group are settled down and start to look expectantly at Dr Hopeful. She decides to get started 'Hello everyone, while we're waiting for the others, can I just remind you about ...' after a couple of minutes of administrative time-filling, she gives up on the others and gets on with the tutorial. 'As you know, today we're going to be discussing ... I asked you all to prepared some draft answers to these questions ... who'd like to start?'. There is an uncomfortable silence. Dr Hopeful continues with a recap of what she hoped they would consider in answering the questions, then turns to a student who is usually keen: 'Nasreen, how did you tackle the first question?'. The others hide their sighs of relief while Nasreen stumbles through a few points and then falters. It's 9.20. The door bangs open and two more students come in, apologising for being late and making a bit of a fuss about finding seats and settling down. Dr Hopeful sighs and turns back to Nasreen. She recaps Nasreen's points and then starts to develop them. The students jot down notes and listen carefully. Although Dr Hopeful tries again to get the students to take a more active role by asking questions, the rest of the hour somehow passes with a recap of last week's lecture on the topic. The following week, there are a couple fewer students present, and they seem to have done even less preparation.

It doesn't have to be like this. Working with small groups can be one of the most rewarding aspects of a lecturer's role. The performance element of a lecture is removed, and there is an opportunity for students and tutor to get to know each other. The mass of the lecture group separates into individuals, each of whom will have their own way of moving through the course and will need different forms of support. In a small group, it is much easier to find out which students are lacking in confidence, who has flashes of brilliance, who will diligently complete all tasks on time, who is struggling to keep up, who is juggling multiple responsibilities and who frequents the bar.

The traditional ideal of small group work is the Oxbridge tutorial, in which one or two students present their work for criticism on a weekly or fortnightly basis. This approach can be effective in two main ways: by honing the student's writing style until it conforms to the tutor's expectations and, secondly, by providing continuous feedback to the tutor about the student's knowledge and understanding. The first is ideal if the assessment of the award is based on writing essays, and the second is always useful to the tutor, but both purposes can be achieved in other ways if needed. Modern higher education is seldom resourced to provide one to one interaction, but the Oxbridge model works because of a clear understanding of responsibilities: the student will write an essay and the tutor will read and critique it. There are rewards for doing well (the tutor gives praise) and sanctions for not doing the work (the tutor is displeased).

For the students, small group work is a chance to test out their ideas in a safe environment, ask for help, develop their skills in discussion, debate, and constructing argument, and to discover that tutors don't have all the answers to academic questions. The chance to build individual relationships is one of the things most people enjoy about teaching in HE.

Small group work may be regularly scheduled (eg weekly tutorials) or may occur for particular projects or during field trips or visits. The role of the academic is more akin to that of a team leader or co-ordinator in the workplace, rather than imparting knowledge. The tutor may take responsibility for planning, setting boundaries and monitoring progress, but the aim should be to get participation and meaningful work from the rest of the team. The role is challenging: there need to be ground rules; there need to be rewards for being part of the team and sanctions for not participating; students need to buy into the idea of team working rather than passive listening. The rewards might be an obvious feeling of group endeavour (and participation marks); the sanctions could be a feeling of letting the group down, or be driven by assessment concerns (not earning the participation marks).

The starting point should be to decide what each tutorial or set of tutorials should achieve: is it for students to

- learn in more depth about a topic?
- apply something they've learned to another situation?
- show that they can construct a particular kind of argument?
- think through the consequences of a particular set of actions?
- show that they can develop critical questioning skills?
- apply a skill such as producing a *précis* of an academic paper?

In general, planning should be about process-oriented outcomes: subject knowledge can be acquired elsewhere (lectures, libraries, digital sources). Small groups are one of the few situations where there can be meaningful interaction and where direct feedback can be given to students about their skills development. Faced with silence, or lack of preparation, resist the temptation to run a mini-lecture. Students may be too aware of their lack of knowledge or preparation, or too nervous or reluctant to talk about the topic in front of the tutor, who is already the expert. Using a variety of tasks in tutorials will keep everybody challenged and should make the sessions more enjoyable, as well as giving varied personalities opportunities to shine. Have a backup plan: if someone is ill or hasn't done the preparation, you need to have an alternative activity ready.

Figure 4.2 gives some ideas for small group work. Like most tools of the teaching trade, it takes a while to feel comfortable with using a variety of approaches

---

Figure 4.2: Tutorial ideas

- Debates
- Student-led introduction to topic followed by discussion
- Considering ideas or concepts from different perspectives, such as 'If I were a behaviourist, how would I interpret this event?' or 'In this situation, what would the project manager do? How about the HR director?'
- Approaching the topic from an unusual angle, such as asking small groups to pictorially represent the concepts they are considering and discussing the results
- Role playing
- Group problem-solving tasks
- Working on mathematical or technical problems alone, with the benefit of the tutor present to answer questions

---

to small group teaching. Some sessions will be more successful than others, but it is worth persevering to find the styles that work well for tutor and subject.

Small group work may also take place in laboratories or practical workshops. In that case, many of the same principles apply, but the purpose of the session is likely to be more tightly constrained than for the examples in Figure 4.2.

Marking

When we ask new lecturers how marking makes them feel, around 70 per cent use words like 'stressful', 'worrying' or sometimes 'responsible'. Actually, experienced lecturers often feel like this too. It is a lot of responsibility, and people quite rightly feel under pressure to mark competently and confidently. Unfortunately, in some departments there is little discussion about marking, nor is there usually much training or staff development available. There seems to be an assumption that people will know how to do it from having had their own work marked in the past, or perhaps that marking is simple enough for guidance to be unnecessary. This section is intended for those who are thrown in at the deep end, as many of us were when we started teaching in HE and focuses on marking assignments which have already been set.

> Students can, with difficulty, escape from the effects of bad teaching, they cannot ... escape the effects of poor assessment. (Boud, 1995)

Getting started

When a batch of scripts to mark is received it is vital to have to hand the assignment brief, details of the assessment criteria being used and some information about feedback policy. Firstly be clear what the assignment brief/question is asking for – this can be easier said than done. You might jot down a couple of possible outline solutions and think about what an excellent assignment might look like. If a model answer has been provided by the person who set the assignment, you have a standard for comparison. Next, use the assessment criteria to give the outlines rough marks and think about how the criteria could be interpreted. This helps you get your bearings before starting to look at students' work.

The deadline to get the assignments marked must be met. Make a sensible marking timetable and stick to it, but do leave enough time for breaks, and don't mark too many in one sitting. It's unfair to the students if the tutor becomes too tired and fed-up to concentrate.

It is a good idea to skim through the submissions to be marked and group them roughly according to quality. Assignments may be reallocated in this rough grouping when read more thoroughly, but it can be easier to mark several assignments of similar level sequentially. Having a good sense of an excellent assignment makes it easier to pinpoint problems in the rest, so begin with those which appeared from the first skim through to be the best.

Policies on correcting presentational and linguistic errors may vary between departments. The most common approach is to correct one or two of the same type of error and then to underline similar errors. But it is important to be consistent with what colleagues do, as students will find it troubling if different people approach marking differently.

To achieve the purpose it is intended to serve, written feedback should concentrate on what the student needs to do to improve their technique, knowledge or future approach. What would have lifted the assignment up a grade? How does what they did in this assignment relate to assignments which will be set later or elsewhere in the programme? It is helpful for the tutor as well as the students to know where individual assignments fit in the bigger scheme of things.

It is tempting to write feedback to justify the mark, or to produce a list of things that students did not do in the assignment, but such approaches will not help students to move on very far. To justify the mark, a marking grid may be helpful (such as the example in figure 4.3) to highlight the criteria used in the assessment and to show where improvements can be made.

Students who have done well need feedback as much as students who have room for improvement. They have invested time in getting it right. Highlighting elements which were particularly good will help them to know what kinds of areas to develop further next time.

The language of feedback is also critical to student development: positive formulations such as 'next time, try to ...' are more encouraging than phrasing such as 'you didn't ...' or 'you should have ...'. This isn't a matter of being politically correct: the mark will show them when they have done badly. It is a matter of approaching feedback in a way which shows awareness that they can improve and giving them some concrete suggestions for doing so. Students will generally have put a lot of work into their assignments and may find it difficult to absorb criticism about something in which they have considerable personal investment.

Figure 4.3: example of a marking grid

	Academic Context	Relationship of theory to practice	Critical evaluation	Structure and Presentation
85-100	Outstanding use of relevant sources, showing an exceptional range of reading and understanding of current practice in and beyond their own subject area.	Outstanding level of independent and creative thinking which links theory and practice. Excellent integration of theory into the task.	Exceptionally high level of critical insight and evaluation, sophistication and accuracy. Identifies all implications of critique and is autonomous, original and challenging. Persuasive arguments which generate new perspectives.	Clear, concise, fluent and well structured work. Could be considered for publication. No errors in citations, quotations or referencing.
70-84	Excellent use of relevant sources, showing evidence of a wide range of reading and understanding of current practice at least in their own subject area.	Excellent links between theory, practice, and the assignment task.	Excellent level of independent and creative thinking. Well formulated arguments which may generate new perspectives.	Clear, concise, fluent and well structured work. No errors in citations, quotations or referencing.
60-69	A good summary of the principal issues, gained from a good range of reading and understanding of current practice at least in their own subject area.	Good links between theory, practice, and the assignment task.	Identifies strengths and weaknesses of material. Clearly formulated arguments.	Clearly structured work. No or few grammatical errors. Referencing of good quality. Quotations used appropriately.

Figure 4.3: example of a marking grid (continued)

	Academic Context	Relationship of theory to practice	Critical evaluation	Structure and Presentation
50-59	A sound summary of the principal issues, showing evidence of use of basic course material and awareness of current practice.	Some links between theory, practice, and the assignment task.	Some evidence of independent critical thinking. Arguments may need further development.	Understandable structure. No or few grammatical errors. Referencing and use of quotations adequate.
45 to 49	Insufficient evidence of knowledge of the principal issues with little reference to literature or relevant current practice.	Poor links between theory, practice, and the assignment task. Some links may be present but the integration is insufficient.	Descriptive writing which doesn't identify strengths and weaknesses of material. No attempt to create new perspectives.	Poorly structured. Referencing inaccurate, inadequate and/or irrelevant. Too many quotations used.
<45	Little or no relevant material.	No links between theory, practice, and the assignment task.	Descriptive writing with no critical thinking about the topic.	Poorly structured. Referencing mainly inaccurate, inadequate and irrelevant. Too many quotations used.

Check the working

After marking a reasonable range of student work, it can be useful to discuss some sample assignments with a colleague. Ideally, it would be the person who has set the assignment, or someone else marking the same assignment if it is a marking team, or another experienced marker. But talking to anybody else marking work in the same discipline at a similar level would help. Many departments have double-marking systems where academics are paired to review scripts, or moderation schemes where a colleague moderates a sample of the marked work. These approaches provide good opportunities to discuss expectations and any difficult decisions.

There is research to show that marking is not an exact science, and that both experienced and inexperienced markers will give the same assignment different marks in different situations (Ecclestone, 2001; Hanlon, Jefferson *et al*, 2004), as well as there being variations between disciplines and institutions (Yorke, Bridges *et al*, 2000). Academics new to marking need to be sure they have fully understood the level that is required and that they are comfortable in explaining their marking decisions, so talking to more experienced colleagues is invaluable. As tutors become more experienced, and once they set their own assignments, there may be less need to do this, but even after over forty years between us of marking, we appreciate working in teams which discuss marking decisions.

Accurate recording of marks, in a spreadsheet, mark sheet or online entry system is as critical as getting the marking right. A good approach is to read out the marks from the assignments to a willing friend or colleague who is checking them on the master summary. This is particularly important when anonymous marking is used and students are identified by number – it is usually more difficult to link numbers than names with marks reliably. This may sound like a trivial detail but can save hours of checking at the time of examination boards.

Researching

Conducting research is a key area of academic activity. Although not always a required part of the role, it is useful for two reasons – firstly for keeping academics up to date with things happening in their discipline and secondly for enhancing their employability and career development. People new to academia may feel this is a step too far at the start of their career but it is a good idea to begin at once to think about it. This section looks at how to get started, the support which may be available and how to find funding.

Many staff still come into HE from a traditional apprenticeship background of research degree followed by post-doctoral research. Those who have taken this route will probably find that they are already sufficiently skilled in the basics of research and that the difficult part of continuing to do research is trying to balance all the additional commitments that come with teaching and administration.

However, the apprenticeship is no longer the only route into becoming a full-time member of academic staff, and many lecturers are now appointed for their expertise and experience in their professional area. Those coming into HE from professional practice may feel a little daunted by the prospect of beginning to do research in their subject and because formal research may not be a required part of their role, it can be easy to avoid getting involved by focusing on other areas. However, it is worth making an effort to do some research and scholarly activity in addition to teaching and administration. Studying or developing an area in more depth increases confidence in tackling the supervision of under-graduate projects and teaching on post-graduate degrees. In addition, keeping up to date and enthused in the discipline has a positive impact on teaching.

For those who do not already have a post-graduate qualification, undertaking one is an obvious way in to scholarly activity. Most institutions will be keen to support a member of staff embarking on a first post-graduate course. Choosing an MRes (Masters by Research) or a Masters which has a substantial dissertation/project element will provide a route offering appropriate support. For those already qualified to Masters level, a part-time PhD can be a suitable route, but time and support must be in place for the sustained effort this will demand. For those who already have a post-graduate qualification, or cannot get support from their institution, there are still opportunities to get involved in research by talking to colleagues about what they are doing, asking how to get involved, starting in a small way and then taking more responsibility. All research projects involve leg-work and doing some of it is a good way of finding out more about the basic processes involved in disciplinary research. Setting targets over a four or five year period, such as being acknowledged in colleagues' research, being a named author on a grant application or paper or presenting at a conference is a good way to develop a research portfolio.

As an alternative to discipline-based research, research in teaching and learning is a growth area. Again, formal qualifications or joining a local team are the easiest way to get started, but it may be necessary to look further afield. Most institutions have a centre for learning and teaching or education development, and may know of internal teams seeking new members or of internal funding for small projects. There may also be work linked to a Higher Education Academy Subject Centre (see Chapter two). These often have small grant schemes to help early researchers in learning and teaching, and organise relevant workshops and conferences.

People who come to academic life in mid-career often feel nervous about launching themselves into research, however experienced and talented they are in the practice of their disciplines. It is true that they may need to learn a new set of skills for problem-solving, analysis and evaluation, but it is unlikely that these will differ greatly from the skills they have had to develop to be successful in their working life. While we feel willing to learn something new, we will still have plenty to contribute to the production of new knowledge and interpretations of practice. Being honest about inexperience in the research area does not need any apology: enthusiasm is a huge factor in successful research.

Making Funding Applications

Some experienced researchers would say that applying for grants is the most important skill in research (see Chapter two). Research funding is available from a huge variety of sources and in a huge variety of formats, but is not easy to get. Spend time narrowing down the options and work out which sources most closely match the proposed research. As with getting started with research, the best starting point is to see what others are doing in the area and then work from there. Professional bodies in the disciplines will probably carry lists of funding opportunities, and there are also international services such as researchresearch.com which allow searching and filtering of information about funding rounds. These services are usually subscription based and library or research department staff will be able to advise on institutional access. In the UK, the Research Councils carry information on their web pages. Health researchers can check the National Institute for Health Research website.

As we discussed in Chapter two, institutions will almost certainly have a research department which can help with putting applications together, particularly when it comes to the mysteries of estimating costs and explaining the meaning of Full Economic Costing and overhead recovery. Chances of success are generally increased by working in partnership with people who already have a track record of successful completion. That might mean collaborating with people in other HE institutions or organisations. Contacts and networks can be developed by joining mailing lists to find out what people are discussing, talking to people at conferences or attending research seminars.

Academic enterprise

The term *academic enterprise* covers a whole range of activities in which the professional skills of academic staff are used for purposes outside the mainstream definitions of teaching and research. In most cases the concept is linked to income generation in addition to government funding and fee income, but it can also include non-profit-making community ventures; we looked at some examples earlier. Sometimes the boundaries between teaching, research and enterprise may be blurred – is a one- day training workshop very different from the same session taught as part of a post-graduate programme? Does a three-day consultancy which analyses the management structure of a small company and makes recommendations differ from a small research case study?

Getting involved in enterprise

The extent to which it is feasible to get involved in enterprising activities will depend on the subject discipline and the general culture in the department. It may be a cliché that certain subjects don't engage much in academic enterprise but it is certainly going to be more difficult if there is no local or national culture of working outside the ivory towers. If there is already activity then the same general approach as for getting involved in research should be effective: for example, offering to support existing activity and gradually developing a niche. For those who have come directly from a professional situation, talking to former contacts about the kinds of collaborative work or consultancy which might be useful in the field could provide some leads. Do they need placement students? Could a small scoping study be useful for them, using the institution's library and other resources? Does something need testing with specialist equipment to which the university has access? For those ploughing a new furrow, trying to find out what other institutions do in the subject area may throw up new ideas.

Institutions have different policies when it comes to approving consultancy and enterprise arrangements and deciding on costs. Some institutions will take over the whole thing from arranging contracts to invoicing for completed work, while others will leave it to the academics. As with research funding, it is a good idea to make contact with the relevant people early on to clarify the limits of possible commitment. An enterprise office will be able to advise about negotiating contracts, and calculating costings, overheads, fees, and timescales. Most institutions will have some arrangement for profit-sharing on enterprise contracts; payments may be made directly to academic staff, either personally or to a personal research fund, or they may be absorbed into departmental costs. These arrangements may influence any decisions to engage in new activity so should be identified early in the planning process.

It is important to be clear who owns the intellectual property or copyright on any materials or resources produced as part of the activity. If involved in original research for an external client, there needs to be agreement on what they will allow to be published in peer-reviewed journals or used in future research. There may be confidentiality clauses, or they may want to use the work for other dissemination activity of their own. Establishing parameters from the outset can prevent disputes arising and legal agreements or contracts may need to be prepared by the university's solicitors.

Supporting students

The diversity of students in higher education today means that we cannot make any assumptions about their expectations of university life nor about their ability to integrate into the HE community. Cohorts have generally become larger, making a personal approach more difficult. To try to cover all the possibilities, institutions and course teams tend to produce thicker and thicker information packs for new students. However, an individualised approach may be possible if the course team aims for preparing the students to live and work as a community which can find information when it is needed rather than being handed all the information in a difficult-to-digest lump. This section makes suggestions for working in this way.

Pre-entry and induction

Student support starts before the beginning of the first term. Most universities now try to build relationships with their incoming students as soon as an offer has been accepted. Usually, the marketing department begins this initiative, but as the start date nears, the programme team will be responsible for preparing information to be sent out and for planning pre-entry and induction activities. Pre-entry and induction support from the programme team is about welcoming and inducting students into the academic community. It provides an opportunity to prepare students for what is expected of them during their courses, to introduce individuals and to flag up important sources of help and support which may be needed if the going gets tough.

Those responsible for any teaching in the first year will probably be asked to contribute to pre-entry materials and induction planning, so think about what purpose this material can serve. For decades pre-entry has been characterised by sending out handsome leaflets, colour-coded papers and induction programmes, but there has been very little study of the usefulness of such information. Recent studies carried out as part of an HEA-funded project (Dawson *et al*, 2009) found that students did not remember having seen pre-entry information such as timetables, even though such information was definitely in the packs sent out. Some students may have found it overwhelming, others might have read it all but found it too much to take in, others will have skimmed through it and found it difficult to work out what to prioritise.

The Student Transition and Retention Project at the University of Ulster has done interesting work on transition into HE and suggests that

> 'Induction must be seen as a set of processes (not an event) that introduces students to:
>
> ■ a higher education institution as an academic community
>
> ■ their campus as a distinctive social organisation and centrally based support services
>
> ■ their Faculty as an organisational unit
>
> ■ their programme of study and the academic framework in which they will learn
>
> ■ the academic staff who will deliver the course and assess their performance
>
> ■ their peer group (Cook *et al*, 2005)

One institutional framework for pre-entry and induction (MMU, 2009) suggests that teams should be able to provide:

> ■ detailed knowledge of course content, including course options and units
>
> ■ an indicative timetable
>
> ■ information on how students will be assessed
>
> ■ guidance on what the key texts will be in first year

These are all practical elements that will enable students to plan ahead, particularly in terms of timetabling and assessment requirements for students who have other commitments too. The institution will provide general information about financial support, accommodation, campus facilities, support services, support for disabilities and so on. It is tempting to simply assemble a pack of documents, but what matters is what the recipient does with each item.

The characteristics of the student cohort and particularly their familiarity with HE should determine the style, tone and quantity of material to be despatched. Some of it could probably be held back until arrival, or be provided online, followed by a personal introduction from the course team which reassures students they don't have to memorise everything at once, as help will be available when they need it.

Pre-entry and induction are essential components in confirming the student in their choice of course and preparing them to embark on that programme as soon as they arrive. Many students who leave HE in the first year do so because they felt that they had chosen the wrong course (Yorke and Longden, 2007) or because they had difficulty in integrating socially or academically. So pre-entry and induction activities should link the introduction to the first sections of the course and provide some socialisation activities for students and staff.

Social networking sites

Many departments and courses use social networking sites to welcome new students. There has been some debate about adults interfering in younger people's social spaces, but informal arrangements can work well, particularly if they are moderated by existing students rather than staff. A quick search of Facebook will show what other courses and universities are doing (just search for an institution or course title). Most universities have a Twitter site as well, but these tend to provide marketing updates. For a larger course, a regular Twitter feed could suggest what enrolling students should be considering or give interesting information about the course. Some institutions are also trying out Second Life to provide a virtual introduction to campus life. But failing to update these activities regularly could send out the wrong signals to the soon-to-be community members.

Preparation work

If students are unlikely to have encountered a subject in their previous studies, sending them some introductory study work in advance will help confirm their interest. Lists of suggested pre-reading are fairly traditional, but rather uninspiring and unguided reading does not always give students a sense of what will be expected of them. More effective is a study guide accompanying a reading list, or an online quiz to complete before arrival, or questions set for small groups to study online or to link specific induction activities to the reading.

Games and simulations

Games and challenges are now being used to help build communities. These are tackled on campus when students arrive, or done at a distance as an internet searching exercise, to be completed individually or in teams. Treasure hunts – simple paper-based exercises or more sophisticated role-playing games – which use clues to encourage students to find out more about the local area or a particular course (Whitton *et al*, 2008).

Induction activities

Here's a thought. Put a few hundred excited, anxious people who don't know each other in a lecture theatre for three hours while a succession of important people tells them a great deal of important information that they must try to remember for the next three years. Although this may be fulfilling the obligation to pass on all this information to students, there is little chance that they will take it all in. Better to concentrate instead on the transition to higher education, socialisation with peers and staff, some sample study activities and reassurance that help will be available when needed. Doing things together will help to set students up for their first few weeks – for example a small group discussion of an element of academic skills development, tackling such questions as: *What does a good essay look like? How can you find relevant information from the library? How can I develop my self-assessment skills?*

> At a Law School, new under-graduate students discuss a sample real-life case in what will be their tutor groups. The present case considers the difference between a well known potato-based snack and potato crisps, which has serious VAT implications, but each year brings the possibility of new topical and quirky issues. The groups come to a decision, and then attend a social event with their tutors, with the well known potato-based snack and crisps being served for empirical comparison.

Evaluating and monitoring pre-entry and induction

The best way to ensure that pre-entry and induction activities have been effective is through continuously building on student feedback. Asking students how effective their experiences of pre-entry and induction have been in helping them to integrate into the HE community may benefit future intakes. What will help students to remember elements that were useful and highlight what they needed more information about? Most students need at least a term to settle into university life so drip-feeding information in manageable portions or repeating essential information more than once is advisable. Asking them to confirm their understanding or what are unclear about may seem excessive but is worth the effort.

Pastoral care

Many academic staff feel uneasy about pastoral care. Where does the academic tutorial role end? Lending a friendly ear could lead to requests for support which an academic may be ill-equipped to deliver. A member of academic staff is probably the first person students approach if they have a problem, or the one who identifies a problem when scanning attendance records or marksheets. Therefore, a tutor needs to be prepared to accept disclosure of problems and to be sympathetic. It is part of building and maintaining a relationship with the student cohort.

However, one of the unspoken skills of pastoral work is knowing one's own limitations in supporting students and when a student needs to ask for help from someone more appropriate. Whilst most students of all ages will be able to catch up on a missed lecture here, and a poorly prepared tutorial there, some students may need additional help and reassurance from specialists. Although the tutorial role is important in supporting individuals who have a crisis of confidence, central learning support services exist in most institutions to provide help with time management, or study and writing skills, so tutors can refer people on. Students who have had particular difficulties to overcome in entering HE, such as those who were looked after children, people from groups with no family tradition of HE, asylum seekers or accident or abuse victims might need specialist help. Students can be referred to a counselling service (most UK universities have their own) for problems which go beyond one-off issues such as a child's illness preventing submission on time, a crisis at work or an unexpected problem at home. A counselling service will be much better placed to support students through major life crises such as bereavement, divorce or redundancy than an individual academic.

Figure 4.4 (overleaf) gives some mini-case studies to show how academic and support staff might interact in supporting students. In each of these cases, the role of the academic has effectively been to direct them to the relevant support staff. The tutor has been crucial in identifying that barriers to learning exist for the student, but they only attempt to intervene when the issues are within their remit; that is, if they are related to learning or teaching. Otherwise they refer the student to the relevant professional help. The huge increase in numbers and the great diversity of the student body mean that the quantity and range of issues students might present are far beyond the capacity of individual academic staff to manage. The student support facility might seem costly and unnecessary to some but it shields academic staff from an onslaught they would struggle to survive.

Figure 4.4: Multiple support needs

David is a white 18 year old in his third week of a BA (Hons) Business Studies. He studied A-levels and scraped the grades to get in during clearing. His teachers thought him capable of getting good grades but everything had come easily to him up to AS and he didn't really try. His loan has not yet come through and his parents are not in a position to support him financially. He was late finding somewhere to live and missed some of induction week. He has missed a couple of classes, lost his timetable and has decided he might as well not bother coming in any more.

One of his tutors notices he has been missing and sends for him to try and get him back on track. Once he has unearthed the problems, he directs David to the Student Services Department to discuss his financial situation. They in turn direct him to the Access to Learning Fund and to the Students Union for welfare advice. His tutor finds David a replacement timetable and works through with him what he has missed and what he needs to do. He then refers David to the local study skills officer for guidance on time management and passes the information on to his personal tutor to arrange follow up meetings.

Samina is an 18 year old second generation British Bangladeshi with good grades at A-level who is half way through the first year of a law degree. She is desperately unhappy because she really wanted to study Sociology but her parents would only allow her to come to university to study a 'proper subject'. She has to live at home and her father drops her off each day and picks her up in the afternoon so she can't socialise with other students. She shares a room with three siblings and has to do work around the house, so she finds it difficult to study and has already fallen behind with her coursework.

Her personal tutor notices that she started off very strongly but is slipping back, so arranges a tutorial to discuss her work. Having elicited the facts of the case from Samina, her tutor realises it is too complex for her to resolve herself, so makes an appointment for Samina with a Senior Adviser in the Student Welfare Department. She asks Samina to come and see her later in the term to see how things are going.

Jenny is 34 and has two small children. Her older child (6) is at school and the younger (18 months) in the university nursery. She is in the second year of a Psychology degree and has been getting consistently high grades, suggesting she is likely to get a first class degree. She loves her course and is a good student (attends punctually, meets deadlines, engages in group work and reads beyond the course materials). But she has been in receipt of Access to Learning fund support and this has suddenly stopped. The nursery has announced it is closing and she has had to take her son out of after-school care. She is desperate to continue the course but the financial problems are putting a lot of strain on her marriage.

Jenny makes an appointment to see her personal tutor to try to get help. Her personal tutor refers her to the welfare department in the Students Union to get advice on her financial support entitlements. He goes through Jenny's timetable with her to see whether switching to alternative tutorials would allow her more flexibility to collect her son from school. He refers her to the university's student employment scheme which provides paid work for students to

> fit with their study patterns and suggests she seek additional support from the university counselling service.
>
> **Danny** is a Chinese post-graduate undertaking a PhD in Chemistry. His first degree is from a Chinese university and he has spent six months in England at a language school. His parents have borrowed huge amounts of money to get him here but he is still struggling with the language, is very lonely and has been feeling unwell. He thinks he is doing OK with his studies and does not realise he is depressed.
>
> His supervisor has noticed that he seems to spend every waking hour in the labs but is not making much progress. She arranges a meeting to discuss this with him and manages to persuade him to make an appointment with a university counsellor.

In the UK and elsewhere, universities are required by law to make reasonable adjustments for disabled students (see Chapter three). But academic staff are not expected to provide the sole support for the disabled student – there are relevant central services with which tutors can work to establish reasonable adjustments. Adjustments such as releasing handouts in advance often benefit the whole group, so adaptations can be seen as positive elements to the course.

Students from diverse backgrounds bring enrichment to a cohort and so planning teaching and support should allow for a wide range of approaches and responses. Remaining flexible is a good way to be prepared for all kinds of changes.

Administration

> Sally rushes into the regulation review committee ten minutes late, clutching lecture notes and apologising to the Chair. The person speaking pauses while Sally settles into her seat and digs the meeting papers out of her bag, then does a quick recap for Sally's benefit. Sally is aware of other people looking at her. She seethes a bit. She was lecturing until the meeting start time! What is she supposed to do when a student keeps her back and asks her questions? She only comes to this committee to ensure there is academic representation. Administrators just don't understand... On the other side of the table, the faculty quality officer feels a bit sorry for the obviously stressed Sally, but wonders why she didn't just say she would be late, or declined to sit on the committee if this would clash with her teaching?

Academic administration is an essential and inescapable part of the academic role. It covers a huge variety of tasks and the nature of what is required varies between institutions more than any other aspect of the academic role. Administration can involve noting and sorting attendance registers; entering marks; timetabling; chasing up non-attenders; dealing with admissions and recruitment; serving on committees and working groups; exam boards; departmental meetings; reviewing policy documents; contributing to strategy ... the list is long. Most members of academic staff get more enjoyment from the teaching, research and enterprise elements of their jobs, but the administrative elements are essential to keep all these aspects running smoothly. It is vital for academic staff to understand and engage with the administration just as it is for administrators to understand the role of academic staff. Getting the balance right over who does what is not always easy and it is not always successful.

When joining a department, time and effort will be saved by getting to know the administrative staff, and finding out what they do and what they need from academic staff in order to do their jobs. Administrative and academic staff work best as a team. Most of us have ended up doing administrative tasks simply because we didn't know someone else had the skills and capacity to do it, or because we left it too late to delegate. Spending time talking to administrative colleagues is a worthwhile investment.

Summary

This section set out to help those new to academic life to tackle the core elements of an academic job effectively and prioritise their work in the first months as an academic. As confidence grows and further responsibilities are taken on, opportunities to enhance the content and delivery of courses and become involved in other aspects of academic life increase. Chapter five looks at developing additional techniques within a currently approved curriculum, and Chapter six discusses designing new curricula.

5
Working with students

The websites and applications discussed in this chapter are listed in the references.

Introduction

Students in the 21st Century enter higher education for various purposes and they hope for and expect different things. Teachers in HE have to find appropriate ways of supporting them, whilst also ensuring that they can achieve the aims and standards we set for our courses.

How can teaching and assessment be adapted to the needs of the new student? How do we, the teachers, move from being a sage on the stage to being a guide on the side? In Chapter four, we looked at working with the traditional teaching structure. This chapter is about the options available when there is freedom to rework module teaching arrangements. It discusses ways to work with groups, how to use technology to support learning, teaching and assessment, and how to relate academic work to the world outside higher education.

Group work

We have talked about working with small groups in the classroom. Groups of students are also expected to work together on substantial tasks which may be assessed. Being able to work well in a team is a skill most people need in their working lives, but students often find collaborative working difficult. Some report feeling that their own contribution has not been properly recognised when group marks are allocated for assignment work. They also worry about the group failing or some members not contributing to preparation but just turning up for a final presentation. Such feelings may be exacerbated if students feel they are being asked to work in groups so as to reduce the tutor's marking load or relieve timetabling pressures rather than to help them develop particular skills. To make group work a positive experience, it must be carefully planned and supported.

Setting a group task may be a good idea if the intended outcomes for the module involve any of the following areas:

- researching, analysing information and preparing summaries for peers
- agreeing a collective outcome
- managing time effectively, setting deadlines and managing outcomes within deadlines
- accepting and fulfilling agreed responsibilities among peers
- giving and receiving feedback from peers

Planning and preparing group work

The first thing to think about is what kind of tasks would be suitable for collaborative working. A task needs to be able to be divided up into sub-tasks. Ideally, the students should be able to develop and apply individual strengths and combine them to produce a result which represents more than the sum of the contributions. If students were to prepare a project proposal, for instance, there might be clear roles for a creative thinker, a work planner, someone who can analyse finance, a report compiler and someone who can put together an interesting presentation.

A suitable task for a group

- would be difficult for one person to complete on their own
- can be broken down into meaningful sub-tasks
- provides an opportunity for different roles to be deployed in completing the task
- allows the assessment of process as well as outcomes
- can be completed in the time allocated
- can be monitored and supported by tutors in the time available

Tasks which lend themselves well to these requirements are, for example

- Analysis of a complex working situation
- Case study of a multidisciplinary team
- Problem solving which requires several leads to be followed up
- Organising an event or trip

Allocating students to groups

There has been surprisingly little hard research on the issue of group size in educational settings. Small groups make it difficult for individuals to 'hide' but larger groups have been shown in some non-academic situations to be better at thinking up creative solutions. The general consensus is that a group of 4-6 seems about right. However, to simulate a real-world employment activity with a range of employment roles, such as a creative team in an advertising agency, a team planning a particular event, or a team deciding on the best health treatment plan for a patient, the number of roles entailed should determine the size of the group.

Students could experiment with playing different roles to explore their own strengths and weaknesses in a group situation. This too could determine the group size. The Belbin team-roles list indicates the range of potential roles within a group and can be used as a basis for self-evaluation as well as role-play. The summary descriptions are available from the Belbin Team Roles website.

There are three basic approaches for allocating students to groups:

1. friendship – allowing students to self-select
2. random
3. tutor assignment – based on perceived strengths or weaknesses, for instance, or shared interests, or subject options

Each approach has its advantages and disadvantages.

1. Friendship groups

Although this may be the easiest option for the tutor, it is not always effective to ask students to come back next week and report who is in their group of five. Self-selection doesn't have to be based on friendship or acquaintance, but that's what generally happens if people are left to form their own groups. The principal disadvantage to friendship groups is that when left to themselves, people tend to select others who are like them, so may lack the diversity to be effective in terms of experience and competence. According to Hinds *et al* (2000) 'people strive for predictability' when choosing their work group members, as they seek similarity but also 'a reputation for being competent and hard working, and ... [people] with whom they have developed strong working relationships in the past'. People in friendship groups might struggle to be honest with each other because their studying environment becomes too close to their personal environment. This can be a particular problem if assessment stakes or anxiety levels are high. If the individual's final degree classification is affected by the performance of others in the group, tackling an issue may have to be balanced against damaging a supportive friendship. In addition, this method doesn't reflect real-life working situations, where teams are generally formed according to job role rather than by self-selection.

First year students may not yet know enough people on the programme to form a group easily or to find a group to join. Being the last person to be selected for a team, because you are different, or quiet and unassuming, or just unavoidably late or absent at the critical moment, is something one hopes to leave behind at primary school, so if the friendship method is deployed, it needs to be set up carefully.

Nonetheless, there are situations where students might benefit from self-selection: for instance, final year options where there is a shared interest in a topic, or part-time students who come from different geographical areas, or who are on campus only on certain days. Colorado State University's guidance for students when they choose their own groups suggests that they take into account when they are available to meet, individual strengths and weaknesses, diversity, and commitment (LeCourt and Kowalski, 2010).

Self-selected groups can work as long as they have had a thorough induction into the risks and benefits of self-selection, or have been set up with a structured process of self-evaluation where the students are encouraged to compare their strengths and weaknesses when forming the team.

2. Randomly allocated groups

Students may get a better experience of working collaboratively with a diverse range of colleagues and developing skills of performance evaluation and feedback when randomly allocated to groups. The best way to achieve genuinely random groups is to use tools such as those provided in most commercial virtual learning environments (VLEs).

The class list can be used to do the allocation manually. Taking five names at a time in alphabetical blocks is not truly random: there are likely to be five Astons in one group and five Zhis in another. They might be sisters, or share cultural similarities which reduce group diversity. Sorting the class list via student ID rather than name will mix up the names satisfactorily.

Members of randomly allocated groups can have difficulties getting to know each other and settling to the task. This can be mitigated by providing clear induction and some structured introductory activities.

3. Tutor assigned groups

In a tutor assigned group, students are put together for practical reasons, such as placing all those taking a particular combination of electives together to ease timetabling, or for strategic reasons, such as basing the decision on information relevant to the task and its intended outcomes. A task analysing cultural businesses which requires one group of students to visit a museum, one to go to a football club, one to a club venue and so on, might work best if students are divided up according to whether they already have experience or interest in those areas; their existing knowledge may add to their analysis, or encourage them to take a closer look at the subject.

If the students are well known to the tutor – say a group of final year students taking an optional module – then it may be possible to allocate them to groups based on staff perceptions of their strengths and skills. The criteria need to be clear and open, and provide an opportunity for students to challenge the selections. Students will need the same initial support as the randomly allocated groups to help them get to know each other and settle to work: that is, clear induction and structured introductory activities.

Managing group work

Whilst one of the major purposes of group work is to give students time to work on their team-working skills, it isn't just a matter of lighting the fuse and retiring to a safe distance until the assignment task is submitted. Some induction into group working techniques is essential. In particular, students need to know how to:

- identify and allocate roles and responsibilities
- organise their group and individual time
- determine outcomes and processes to achieve those outcomes

It may be helpful to book rooms for students to use in regular timetabled slots, with someone present to answer questions. A longer task might be staged so that the groups have to regularly submit short items for formative feedback, such as a work plan, a progress report and a report outline, so that progress is monitored.

Some students may feel nervous or embarrassed about sharing their work with others, so reassuring them during the whole class briefing that this is normal and that group work is a good way of developing their confidence allows them to expose their work in a relatively safe situation.

Students need to know that differences of opinion among group members are not unusual and that part of the aim of collaborative working activities is to learn to recognise and manage disagreement. Guidance on resolving conflict and re-focusing on the aims of the task should make the following points:

- recognise the possible reasons for difficulties: such as workload distribution, perceptions about each other's commitment and personality differences
- try to discuss the issue within the group: others in the group will probably be aware of any tension and welcome the discussion
- seek guidance from the tutor if needed
- request further support if the above steps have not helped: don't let the situation deteriorate

Group members need individual access to a member of staff in the case of real conflict or anxiety, and a fall-back option for individual assessment should be available in case a group breaks down irretrievably.

Assessing groups

Group work assessments test different kinds of outcomes from individual assignments and so different types of tasks are normally used. Assessment tasks which are commonly used for group work include:

- Presentation
- Poster
- Debate
- Report
- Exhibition
- Performance
- Event organisation

Group assessment can cause anxiety for students, especially if it counts significantly to the final degree classification. Figure 5.1 opposite shows the options for allocating marks for group work.

The selection of the best approach is based on a variety of considerations. If this is the main task for a 30 credit final year unit, the groups are of mixed ability and the students are unfamiliar with group-work processes, then sharing a mark equally between everyone in the group will trouble the students and could distract them from a focus on the tasks and activities required. Figure 5.2 opposite indicates factors which might be used to determine the assessment strategy.

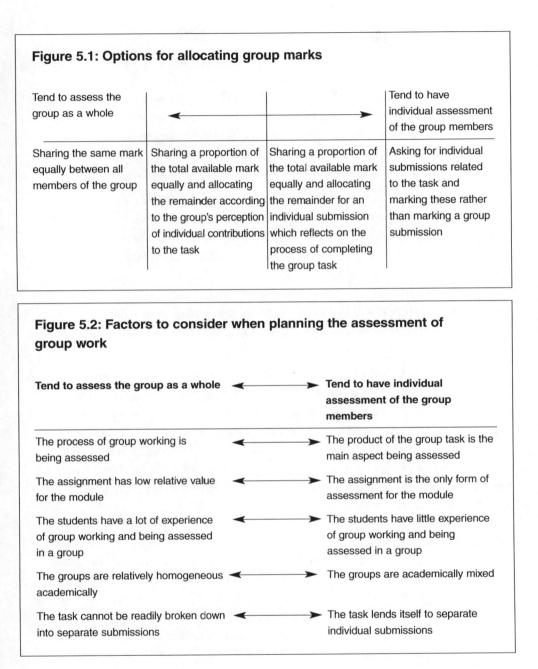

Figure 5.1: Options for allocating group marks

Tend to assess the group as a whole			Tend to have individual assessment of the group members
Sharing the same mark equally between all members of the group	Sharing a proportion of the total available mark equally and allocating the remainder according to the group's perception of individual contributions to the task	Sharing a proportion of the total available mark equally and allocating the remainder for an individual submission which reflects on the process of completing the group task	Asking for individual submissions related to the task and marking these rather than marking a group submission

Figure 5.2: Factors to consider when planning the assessment of group work

Tend to assess the group as a whole	Tend to have individual assessment of the group members
The process of group working is being assessed	The product of the group task is the main aspect being assessed
The assignment has low relative value for the module	The assignment is the only form of assessment for the module
The students have a lot of experience of group working and being assessed in a group	The students have little experience of group working and being assessed in a group
The groups are relatively homogeneous academically	The groups are academically mixed
The task cannot be readily broken down into separate submissions	The task lends itself to separate individual submissions

Using technology

Technology is embedded in higher education teaching in a wide range of ways, varying from course to course and teacher to teacher. Most people will need to experiment to determine the level of technology use with which they are comfortable. This section explores what to think about when adopting particular technologies in teaching. The pace of change means that the technologies cited as examples could be out of date by the time this is read, but the basic selection principles should remain the same.

The fundamental principle is to ensure that the technology is accessible to every student. For working with disabled students, the UK JISC TechDis service provides guides and advice ranging from making electronic documents (eg handouts) more readable to working with students using assistive technology (eg screen-readers). Whilst university campuses may be well equipped, students who need to work from home or their workplace may lack the specialised software. It is therefore critical to identify what students have access to and to establish that they know how to use what is available before investing effort in development.

Technology is well embedded in the HE curriculum and most institutions have a range of basic technology for staff to use for preparing teaching materials and in the classroom. In addition, many free or low cost tools are available which are well adapted for use in teaching – see below. But rapid improvements in software mean that details may soon become out of date. We try as to focus on what can be done with present technology to assist teaching. Information systems services usually provide guidance on the specific technology available in their own institution.

Classroom technology

Classroom technology has changed considerably since the turn of the century. A data projector and linked computer has replaced the overhead projector, allowing the use of software such as Microsoft PowerPoint™ to prepare presentations in advance, and also to show other teaching materials such as videos to the group. A document camera enables real objects to be shown in class, or students to share notes or artefacts. Electronic whiteboards offer the possibility of saving notes made during a session. Each institution has its own classroom set up, so it is best to contact the audio-visual support team or information systems team for support in using the equipment or to find out more about the possibilities. Regular training sessions or one to one support are usually available.

Virtual learning environment

The now ubiquitous Virtual Learning Environment, or VLE, can be used to distribute information of various kinds to students, such as lecture notes, assignment briefs, web links and announcements. Most systems also accept assignments electronically, release computer-marked tests, or host a discussion forum. Training sessions are usually offered for new users, together with downloadable manuals to help with the technical aspects. Look also at the Higher Education Academy (HEA) subject centre resources on using VLEs or at some of the excellent books on the topic such as Salmon (2002).

Texting

Many institutions will have systems in place for sending text messages to students' mobile phones, most commonly for informing them of last minute changes to the programme such as cancelled lectures. But there are costs involved, and students may not be too keen on receiving too many messages from their tutors although they may welcome those which support teaching: for instance, texting out a reminder of the reading for the week after a seminar rather than emailing them.

Web 2.0 applications

Web 2.0 applications such as Blogger, YouTube, Facebook, Twitter, Flickr, wikis and many others are intended to help people to share information and content across the internet. They don't work in the same way or do the same things, but they are often lumped together in conversation or media reports and share similar strengths and weaknesses in the ways they might be used in HE.

Some people think it best not to try to use applications for education which students use for leisure purposes, and that some separation is preferable so that students do not feel that their private systems are being intruded on by teachers. On the other hand, these may be useful tools for gaining and retaining student attention, because the students will be 'there' already. So far, research evidence is based on small scale case studies: there are many examples of successful use of these applications to support learning, but there could be many undocumented attempts which have been less successful.

Blogs

Web Logs, or blogs, are essentially an online diary. They are easy to set up and update, so that people don't need to be IT specialists to have a web site. Students can keep in touch with the blog using so-called 'push' technology (such as an RSS reader – the Google Reader is very easy to use) which delivers updates directly to them rather than their having to log in as for a VLE. A blog could be used for interesting news articles, reminders, digressions, links and reflections, and students can be allowed to comment on blog entries. If comments are allowed, some kind of registration system is needed to check comments before they are posted, as even the most obscure blogs attract advertising and unwanted comments from people who may not have been the intended audience. Registration systems are usually available from free blog hosting services such as Blogger or Blogspot, or a blog tool may be included in the VLE.

Twitter

Twitter works on a similar principle to a blog, as regular updates are sent to a website. It is probably even easier to use, and many modern mobile phones are equipped to connect directly to Twitter, making it available wherever students are. There is a restriction of 140 characters per entry, so it won't work for weighty reflections, and people can't comment directly, although they can tweet back with a Twitter response to an entry.

The example in figure 5.3 shows an extract from a Twitter feed for a level 6 accountancy course.

Figure 5.3: Twitter feed for a final year accountancy module (with thanks to Nick Scott from Manchester Metropolitan University)

■ All coursework is now marked and moderated. It will be posted out this week. If you want some feedback then come and see me. 9:23 AM Dec 15th from Twitterrific

■ There are classes all week. Lectures, super tutorials and support tutorials are as normal. Podcasts will be available for all sessions. 2:36 PM Dec 12th from Twitterrific

■ IASB welcomes decision by Japanese FSA to permit domestic use of IFRSs for current financial year: The IASB wel.. http://bit.ly/5HUcQL 7:19 AM Dec 11th from twitterfeed

■ Trustee letter to G20 participants: The Trustees of the IASC Foundation today issued a letter to participants o.. http://bit.ly/51fk25 9:29 AM Dec 10th from twitterfeed

■ IFRIC publishes proposed guidance on customer loyalty programmes: The draft addresses accounting by entities th.. http://bit.ly/4Gp4x3 5:14 AM Dec 10th from twitterfeed

■ IASB simplifies requirements for disclosure of related party transactions: The IASB has issued a revised versio.. http://bit.ly/7f8f58 3:29 AM Dec 10th from twitterfeed

---

The Twitter feed is used here for a mixture of course-related purposes and students can get the information via Twitter itself or it is copied directly into their VLE for those who prefer to go and look for updates rather than have them 'pushed' at them automatically.

A simple rule for using this kind of application is to do it so there is some separation from everybody's normal life, by creating a special account used only for course-related materials. A Twitter feed for a course can be really useful for giving students regular updates on what is happening, both on the course and with related current affairs. But students won't want it to be mixed up with a personal feed which fills them in on a tutor's social life.

Using existing material

The internet makes it easy to find and locate existing materials in a wide range of formats, and these can help to change the pace in a session, demonstrating the relevance of a topic, engaging students or introducing a task. The challenge for tutors is to select from the huge range of material available.

Many useful free teaching resources are available, from online lectures to animations which illustrate scientific principles, to ideas for session plans. It can be hard to sift through everything on offer. The UK HEA subject centres have links to good resources which have already been filtered by subject specialists. Repositories of shareable teaching materials JORUM in the UK and MERLOT in the US are well worth a look.

Flickr is a good source of still photographic images. The copyright on individual images varies between users so must be checked. FreeImages and Free DigitalImages both have a range of quality photos. Google Images can be used to find photos and other images. Much of what is there is copyright protected so permissions need to be checked carefully.

TASI, the JISC Advisory Service for digital media, and Intute have created a tutorial on locating images for learning and teaching. As well as finding the images, TASI covers issues of copyright and has a useful links basket which can be used to save links during the session, to be collected at the end.

Some people play audio clips as students come into a lecture in an attempt to create a difference in environment between outside the lecture room and inside. The sound doesn't have to be music, although it usually is. Try using bird song, or 'mystery' sounds related to the topic – the lecture could open with the question 'what do you think that sound was?' Institutions may have a licence from the relevant performing rights society which covers their country. Under this licence legally purchased music or other audio clips can be played in the lecture theatre. Free music and other sound files can also be obtained from the sites listed at the end of the book, among others. All these sites have fee paying services and some free clips.

Film or TV clips provide a good introduction or a change of pace but permissions are restricted. In the UK, check the FAQ on the Educational Recording Agency website for more information. The Film and Sound Archive has a large collection of old but interesting short films which can be used for educational purposes. These sites all provide information about how to cite and reference their sources.

Creating new material

Supporting material such as photographs, or short video or audio clips can be created with readily available equipment such as web cams or mobile phones which have cameras and audio recording facilities. Audiovisual services departments of the university may have portable equipment available for loan. Images or clips can be obtained during research activity or workplace visits. Lectures can be recorded for students to watch or listen to again later, or clips can be produced to cover additional material, such as an explanation of a point students have found difficult, or to provide generic assignment feedback.

Students may also be encouraged to produce and share material as part of the module activities. Town planning students might collect an album of pictures of street furniture and then vote on the best and worst situated examples, offering a token prize for the photographers whose images win the categories; design students might film some vox pops in the local high street on people's attitude to a particular item; history students could be challenged to find or create an image which has an unusual link to the topic being covered. This also provides a good opportunity to cover copyright issues and the ways in which the work of others should be used and acknowledged. If students are going to be taking photographs in public places, they must know about the legal restrictions imposed by the UK's counter-terrorism laws.

Photos can be shared using services such as Flickr or Facebook. YouTube is a free service for hosting videos and can be both a useful source of material and somewhere to put videos made specially to support a course. The iTunes service can be used for audio, and allows students with Apple phones or music players to subscribe to all the material for a particular subject or course. Institutions may have alternatives to these services in place and the information systems or audio-visual services should be able to provide guidance. If a team of people is sharing material, everything should be tagged to help to keep track: a common approach is to use the module code, as shown in the Twitter example in figure 5.2. If more than one person is twittering about the module, the tag allows people to find all entries relating to that tag.

Wikis

Sharing artefacts such as photographs and video clips develops students' creativity and wikis provide a way for a group to create something substantial. Like blogs, wikis are websites which can be set up and updated by non-specialists but unlike blogs, whatever is there can be edited by any authorised user. Wikis can allow students to work collaboratively to build up an assign-ment or add material to an initial starting point. If students are allowed to edit the material, however, there is the possibility for things to move in directions the tutor did not intend. Material which seemed important might be deleted, or inappropriate comments added. Administrative rights over the wiki need to be retained by the tutor, so she has a complete record of the history of any changes and so a previous version can be retrieved if necessary. Having a named login can reduce editing difficulties, although anonymity can be use-ful when dealing with a sensitive topic – in which case, regular checks will be needed to moderate the contents. Most wiki software sends the administrator automated emails when anything is changed. If changes are numerous, they can be filtered into a separate email folder for checking at convenient times without cluttering up the main inbox.

Introducing new technology to colleagues

That the teaching and learning environment is in a constant state of change is due partly to the societal reasons we described in Part one, but it is also due to the rapid evolution of technology. It is interesting that higher education retains a reputation for being distant from the real world and its distractions, whereas in reality it has eagerly adopted technology so as to extend and develop communications with students, improve research tools and support administration. As researchers, workers in higher education often develop technological solutions and support their dissemination into the real world. However, enthusiastic early adoption isn't always a good thing, and there is a history of jumping onto the latest trend and then finding that the economies of scale of wider implementation do not follow.

Paradoxically, many HE staff of all ages are proud to declare themselves to be information technology (IT) illiterate and resistant to major changes in working practices linked to developments in IT. It can be difficult to introduce new approaches but the first step is a reasoned discussion about IT. Implementation of IT, or resistance to it must be based on evidence.

For a start, technology implementation makes sense when it is linked to a real improvement in an area of routine practice. For instance, access to records which allow a personal tutor to see all their students' assignment marks and attendance patterns enables the tutor to deal more effectively with a student they seldom see but who consults them over a specific issue. Classroom technology which allows a tutor to show videos and post up instant feedback from students on the screen may make sessions more relevant and encourage students' attentiveness. Electronic submission of assignments may help part-time students who live away from the campus to work to a deadline. Tutors can share useful links, news items or ideas with a class of students by using social networking tools.

Good places to find out about other examples of this kind of implementation are the JISC website and publications by the Association for Learning Technology. Also HEA subject centres and the many peer reviewed journals which focus on this area such as *Learning, Media and Technology* or the *British Journal for Educational Technology* can be useful sources.

Secondly, the proposed implementation must be properly resourced. As well as equipment and software costs for the basic kit, there are support costs, training and possibly additional support technology (eg shared laptops or computer peripherals). How would a trial be scaled up to cover a larger project? Is this feasible? What would be the implications if an innovation is to be used by all the tutors on a course? How would they be supported?

Small technological innovations such as using a new piece of scientific kit or developing a template for online course delivery based on existing software may be well managed within a course team, but anything that has impact beyond a course is likely to need the full support of an institution's information systems teams. Developing innovative ideas which use technology means working with the service teams as ideas progress. This could bring an interesting and enterprising dimension to a career: working in educational technology is an important role in modern HE.

Real-world situations in the classroom

Academic work is often caricatured as irrelevant to the real world, yet higher education is considered to be an essential preparation for modern working life, and global participation is ever-increasing. This strange tension is often resolved by either bringing the workplace into the classroom or sending students out into the workplace. There are various ways of supporting student learning in these situations.

Case studies

Some academic activity can be based on case studies of real or fictional situations which require students to analyse them in the context of academic theory and evaluate actual outcomes or make their own recommendations for action. Case studies can be based on publicly available documents such as financial statements, court reports, historical records, medical reports, company policies, newspaper articles and so on, or realistic fictional versions can be created. The most common assessment outcome for case study activity is a report.

Problem-based learning

Problem-based learning is rooted in the intention to present students with situations that reflect real life so they learn theory by finding out what they need to know to solve the problem. This approach is predicated on the notion that this is what happens in real working situations. A solicitor starts a case with an interview with a client; a doctor, with a consultation with a patient; a historian, by finding an interesting document or connection; an architect, with a piece of land and a brief. Each then has to find other pieces of information to solve the problem they have to resolve. Using this approach in an academic situation means simulating real situations and encouraging students to identify for themselves what they need to know in order to solve the problem.

With a case study, there may be a clear idea of the answers the students are expected to reach, but with problem-based learning, the work may develop in unpredictable ways. This makes it much more challenging for both tutor and students: it may be difficult to manage the processes students adopt, especially if those methods seem wrong to the tutor, and students may feel unsure about being left to develop approaches and find out information for themselves rather than being told what they need to know. They are also unlikely to be able to guess at the expected answer, and this might be a big change to the way they usually approach coursework. Problem-based learning is often carried out in groups that have been set up in the ways discussed earlier. For assessment, the group might present a design, a diagnosis or a judgement in a written or oral report. To encourage their reflection on process as well as product, they might be expected to present an individual analysis and evaluation of their working methods and their approaches to problem solving.

Simulations

Simulations – an advanced combination of case studies and problem-based learning – are usually staged so that information is provided to the students over a period of time, to model the ways they find out about different elements in a real working situation, or to show how situations naturally develop over time. For instance, in a simulation of a restaurant business, students might receive weekly reports of income and expenditure, customer feedback reports, newspaper reviews, HR reports and so on for the previous week. Simulations are time-consuming to set up and monitor but they can be challenging and engaging for students. Suitable discipline-based simulations may already be available for sharing or purchase – check with the relevant HEA subject centre. Small grants might be available for the development of learning materials or small scale research which could be used to help with the production of a new activity to be shared across the sector.

External speakers and visits

Tutors and students might enjoy the occasional external speaker, be it a colleague with a specialism or somebody from research or industry. A change of scene from the usual lecture theatre or seminar room can refresh the long academic year. When asked to comment on parts of the course they enjoy, students regularly mention these variations. It is a simple and effective strategy for introducing a new topic or bringing one to a close, for disrupting students' routines or enhancing the topic with a specialist or opposing view.

Guest speakers may be chosen for their expertise or strong opinions, or for affording access to situations which a tutor can only describe at third hand. The reasons for inviting them will dictate the preparatory work done with students and the follow-up activities. Students might prepare questions to ask somebody with special knowledge which will help them with a future assignment, or clarify issues they find difficult. This can be followed after the session by discussion about what they learned and how they will develop the issue. If the guest has an unfamiliar or challenging opinion, it is useful to discuss beforehand what makes a good debate, how to react professionally to people whose opinion differs from one's own, and how to analyse arguments critically and respond calmly and clearly. After the session, the debate can be continued through a critique of the arguments.

Off-campus visits allow students to see theory applied in practice and enjoy some social bonding, but they can be difficult to organise, particularly if the department does not traditionally offer them. A risk assessment visit will be needed, and it is advisable to check the terms of liability insurance with the institution's legal department. Compulsory visits must be accessible to all the students – so costs, disabled access, timings for those with caring responsibilities need to be considered. The potential benefits should be balanced against the time needed to set up the activity. A compulsory visit needs to be organised formally, but students can be recommended to go independently to exhibitions, museums or places of interest and report back. Voluntary visits cannot be part of an assessment but can be enriching for those who make them and for those who receive the reports in class.

Work placements

Formal work placements are normally integrated into the curriculum and supported by the course administration. Tutors are usually provided with documentation and there probably will not be much scope for adapting them. Suggestions for introducing accredited work placements are provided in Chapter six.

Accrediting unstructured learning opportunities

In the 1980s full-time students were rarely in paid employment. It is now usual for students to work at least part-time, and there are also many more part-time students in higher education. The requirements of the workplace may divert some attention from study, but these experiences could help to contextualise learning. Giving academic value to the time spent in paid work may bridge the gap between the reduced time for study and providing curricula relevant to future employability. Other activities which are not a compulsory part of the curriculum, such as volunteering or informal work placements, can be counted as valuable experiences.

There are two principal ways in which assignment tasks can be designed to integrate external activities: what Knight and Yorke (2003) refer to as 'claim-making', and 'workplace analysis'. Claim-making asks students to show how required learning outcomes have been achieved. This is a common approach to accrediting prior experiential learning (APEL), allowing students to gain credit for work they have completed before beginning a course of study, but it can also be used with current students. Skills for which students claim achievement may include teamwork, initiative-taking, problem-solving, time management, communications, critical incident analysis and planning. Students usually present a portfolio which provides evidence to support how they can perform in particular roles or tasks.

Alternatively, students could perform some kind of analysis of or in the workplace to gain assessment credit. Students carry out an academic activity using their access to the workplace, for instance students on a business and management course could perform an analysis of their organisation against pre-defined criteria, or critique the organisational business plan. The decision-making structures in a hospital might be studied for a health-related degree, or team-working dynamics for psychology, or resource allocation for an MBA, for instance. This approach brings benefits for both students and the course team: students make effective use of their natural working surroundings, and may even use the activity to gain access to unfamiliar parts of the organisation, and the course is enriched by the examples and practice which are shared. The familiar structure of academic analysis is retained and applied to a real life situation, rather than trying to assess student performance in an uncontrollable external environment.

Involving students in assessment

Students are involved in assessment, completing the tasks set for them and getting tutor feedback on their performance. Self-assessment of their performance is also desirable, so they judge how they may have performed on particular tasks and strive for better marks. The tutor might take account of the opinions of a peer audience when allocating the mark for a presentation, particularly where it counts for only a small proportion of a module mark (Langan and Wheater, 2003). Less formally, students can discuss assignment tasks and give each other feedback on ideas.

It is possible to go further. Do we value accurate self-assessment enough to give students some marks for predicting the mark the tutor gives? Do we consider that another student's judgement on a piece of work could contribute to the final mark for the assignment? Do we trust students to share in marking decisions? These are quite difficult ideas. HE staff might worry that their position as experts could be undermined by sharing an important part of our role with the students. We might distrust assessment decisions if they are not being made by academic staff. And there may be concerns about objectivity: will students give higher marks to their friends?

Involving students in assessment collides with invisible boundaries, but they are worth challenging, whether at the level of individual module or the whole institution. Making accurate and objective judgements about self- and peer-performance is a valuable skill for everyone in the workplace. Arguably, we should formalise its development in the safely-bounded world of higher education in order to prepare students for their future lives.

There is evidence that students who participate actively in assessment have a better understanding of the processes and practices of assessment, and that this can help them to improve their performance in future academic work (Liu and Carless, 2006; Prowse, 2007).

Students can be involved first on a formative basis. To extend it to summative work will require the description of the module in the definitive documentation for the course to be amended. Examples of self- and peer-assessment techniques include:

- getting students to complete their own feedback form and append it to their submission -a percentage of the marks might be given for an accurate self-assessment
- getting students to mark each other's drafts by completing a feedback form and appending it to the submission
- Phil Race has described asking students to estimate their mark for an assignment and then offering them the higher one of his mark or theirs if they differ by less than 5 per cent (Race, 2005)
- Peer assessment of presentations is fairly well-established, with students using the standard form used by tutors. The peer feedback can be used formatively or summatively.

Feedback on assessed work

Tutors are effectively giving students feedback every time they interact with them. Students can be encouraged to identify feedback in different contexts and to understand that feedback is not confined to written comments on their work but occurs in many teaching and learning situations. Ideally, each unit will include some formally scheduled class time where assessment and feedback are explained before assignment deadlines, followed by some interpretation after work has been handed back. However, assignment deadlines may mean that classes are finished before marking can be returned to students.

Examples of different types of feedback are:

- written reports (the classic feedback sheet)
- oral reports (eg recorded on a voice recorder and uploaded into a VLE)
- video reports using a webcam
- tick sheets, where areas for development are highlighted from a generic selection

- use of standardised comments with the help of a software package
- one to one tutorial feedback (eg for dissertation students)
- instant feedback in a practical situation or as part of a teaching activity ('thanks for answering that question' in a lecture, 'watch out that your beaker doesn't overflow' in the lab, etc)
- self-assessment checklists
- generic feedback to a group
- distribution of model answers

This list is not exhaustive nor in any particular order. A long list, together with an indication of the learning reward versus efficiency of system appears in Chapter 5 of Phil Race's book (2005). Reviewing it when thinking about different approaches to feedback is recommended.

It is good practice to indicate which form of feedback will be used in which situations and roughly how much feedback might be expected in each case (eg 60 second audio clip, completed one page checklist). This will depend on the type of assignment: a checklist works well for giving instant feedback after a presentation, but a detailed written report will be needed for a dissertation.

Assessment criteria and feedback plans are unlikely to be the same for each level of an award. For example, it may be more appropriate to focus on the functional and technical aspects of the submission at level 3 (foundation year) than is needed at level 6 (final year).

Timing of feedback

Feedback definitely needs to be timely – provided when the student will benefit most. *Timely* is not synonymous with *fast*. When planning a feedback strategy, look at each type of feedback being used and estimate how long it will take to provide feedback on each assignment for each student. Take into account any technical considerations, such as how long it takes to collect in assignments and distribute them to markers, time needed to upload audio or video files, and so on. An estimate of the expected feedback date should be published in the unit handbook along with the assignment submission deadline. If it looks as though some feedback will take an unacceptably long time to deliver, or place an unacceptable strain on staff, delay might be reduced by

- sharing the marking across the team
- providing some generic feedback to the group after having marked a sample of submissions, which highlights common strengths and

weaknesses (see section on generic feedback and model answers, below)

- carrying out peer marking on the submissions during teaching sessions so that students continue to think about the assignment while the tutor marking is completed

- asking students to carry out a self-assessment so they review the submission after a short break, again so they continue to think about the assignment (see section on engagement below)

The use of generic feedback and model answers

Rather than writing similar comments on many feedback forms, generic feedback can be used to highlight successes and problems common to an assignment and point the whole class towards areas of development. Generic feedback can be easier for students to absorb than individual feedback – especially when they have put in much effort – although some will think this generic stuff cannot apply to them.

Generic feedback can be provided verbally or in writing. It may be most effective during a timetabled session, if the whole class is together and if attendance is good. It just takes 10 minutes to:

- reiterate what was expected from the assignment
- summarise which elements were generally produced successfully – one or two examples of something very good might be mentioned without naming names – the people concerned will know who they are
- summarise any common problems: academic writing skills, missing the point of part of the assignment, poor referencing, etc. To avoid embarrassment, it is best not to give examples
- provide information or links for further development of these areas or indicate where revision is needed
- explain briefly how to use this information to go back over their own work and learn for future assignments
- a one page handout with the same information will be useful to jog memories later, and for the students who did not attend this session

A model answer can be useful for some assignments – for instance where there is a right answer, such as a mathematical problem. For many university-level assignments, however, this will not be the case, and a model answer may cause confusion or anxiety, or encourage formulaic approaches in the next assignment. An outline answer which summarises a possible structure for the assignment and gives examples of the kinds of points that were expected is preferable, although indicating that this is an example of just one of numerous approaches.

Model answers and generic feedback are most useful when the work done on the assignment is still fresh in students' minds. If no extensions were given, this could be within a few days of submission, if there has been time to look at a sample of submitted assignments and prepare an overview. But if extensions have been authorised then the assignment cannot be discussed before the agreed extension date, when everyone's work is in. In this situation students will need to wait longer for generic feedback or model answers.

It is useful to pass on generic feedback to colleagues who will be teaching the same group of students in later terms or years. If they have an idea of the strengths and weaknesses of the group, they can adapt their teaching and assessment focus accordingly, and make connections between work carried out in different modules. Such a link between modules may help students to see how seriously the team takes feedback.

Feedback on exams

Students could learn more from their examination experiences if they receive feedback on their performance. But since examination scripts are not usually returned to students and students are seldom available to receive feedback once marking and moderation are complete, a compromise is to review examination performance with students at the beginning of the new academic year, in a related unit, going over the exam questions and producing model answers for discussion in class.

Enabling students to engage with and reflect on feedback

Seeing feedback sheets gathering dust in the receipting office is frustrating. Even when feedback is collected, tutors do sometimes suspect that students focus more on their mark than on the carefully prepared feedback. Seeing the same mistakes repeated assignment after assignment is also frustrating. If the elements listed above are implemented in a feedback strategy, students will already be receiving useful feedback, but sometimes a little more input is needed for them to apply this feedback to their next assignments.

Firstly, there needs to be a team commitment to feedback and its value. Everyone is putting a lot of time and effort into producing and distributing feedback already, but it may be useful to think about what the team, as well as the students, do with this feedback afterwards. The course team could review student performance in all the assignments undertaken in a year, including examinations. Once marking is complete at the end of the academic year, some generic feedback could be produced to be discussed with classes at the beginning of the next year, which highlights general areas for the class to develop. This also provides an opportunity to introduce the next assignments and relate them to previous ones.

Secondly, some strategies for focusing on feedback in one or two units per year might be tried. For example, marks and feedback could be separated for one assignment, giving feedback one week and the mark the following week. Students may try to predict their mark from the feedback they receive and a bonus 5 per cent for an accurate prediction might encourage reflection. Students submit the predicted mark by a prescribed date; the degree of precision required would be specified (eg to within a degree classification band; or within 5%); the tutor's decision would be final. Time needs to be factored in to compare the list of predictions with the actual marks. This kind of activity might end with a brief class discussion about why the predictions were or were not accurate. This might seem to take classroom time away from the content of the programme, but helping students to engage with the outputs of the unit as well as the inputs will improve their understanding and performance.

When there are two assignments in the same module, some of the marks available in the second assignment could be used to reward students who show how they acted on the feedback in the first assignment. For example, a simple statement might be required at the end of the assignment which explains what they did in response to the previous feedback and indicating where the evidence for improvement can be found in the second submission. Any marks given should be on the quality of the statement rather than their actual improvement, which will be assessed anyway.

Finally, it is important that the course team all share clear ideas about the kinds of language that should be used in feedback and that everyone is primed to 'take care with the important words', as Race (2005) puts it. A course team meeting could review previously issued anonymised feedback and discuss whether or not it used appropriate language. If not, how might it be improved? Figure 5.4 (overleaf) makes some suggestions for trying to rephrase common feedback expressions more constructively.

Students who are performing well may not need as much feedback, but even a good 2(i) grade still leaves at least 31 per cent of marks to be achieved. And

Figure 5.4 Rephrasing feedback in constructive terms

Common phrasing	Improved phrasing
It's a pity you didn't ...	Another thing that you could have tried was...
Your referencing is poor	References must be cited accurately so that readers can follow up your ideas – the library run regular courses and I recommend that you attend one before your next assignment
The assignment was unstructured	Try to develop a stronger structure for your work. There are lots of examples of good structures on the Study Skills website – have a look at those and try to check your structure with a fellow student or a tutor before finishing your next assignment

it is important to reinforce good performance, whether in individual feedback with phrases like 'you approached this task in the right way' or in generic feedback: 'those who did ... performed very well on this assignment'. Students need to be motivated to keep developing; they need to know what would have got them a first class mark. This is also a useful area for discussion amongst colleagues.

Summary

This chapter has explored ways to enhance teaching and assessment within an existing curriculum structure. Not every suggestion will work for all courses or all teaching styles, but they indicate areas where changes might be made without drastically altering course structures. Chapter six looks at the process of reviewing modules for validation or review.

6
Enhancing quality

Introduction

The previous chapters looked at teaching and assessing modules which have been designed and are managed by others. As they become more experienced, academic staff are expected to design their own teaching materials and write assessment plans and feedback strategies, and to get involved with evaluating various aspects of the student experience as part of the cycle of quality enhancement and course development. This chapter suggests approaches for designing courses and programmes to achieve the expectations of students, employers and parents in the 21st century. It is structured in the sequence in which designing a new course or reviewing an existing one might be tackled, but each section can be read alone if only one element of the course is being reviewed.

> Note: In this chapter, 'course' refers to a programme of study which leads to some kind of award, and 'module' refers to a defined section of that course. In the UK, full-time undergraduates usually study modules worth a total of 120 credits per year. The size of module depends on the institution, but 10, 15 and 20 credits are the most usual unit of currency for modules. One module credit equates to roughly 10 hours of student study.

Aims and learning outcomes

Curriculum planning begins with writing aims and outcomes. At the level of a course or programme, the aims and outcomes are broad-brush: what is it that students will do on the course? What should they be able to do when they have finished the course? Put another way, what will they achieve in return for their investment of money, time and effort? Even if the answers to these questions appear self-evident, to the team, clear, meaningful aims and outcomes should be established. Getting them right is not just a matter of ticking boxes on course documentation forms: they will serve as points of reference for the curriculum design, and inform students about what they can expect to achieve.

Course aims

Chapter two considered factors which influence curriculum shape and design, and the macro-level thinking required when deciding whether or not a course should be developed. Start with a mental model of the successful graduate from the course and compare this with students beginning it. What can they do after completing the course? How do they tackle problems? In what ways do they communicate? Do they have particular values? Figure 6.1 shows some examples.

The aims should incorporate the focus and values expressed in the institutional strategic plan. For example, the institution may want to develop capacity in applied research, or to focus on education for the professions, or on widening participation. Course developers should consider how the proposed course relates to these strategic aims.

Figure 6.1 Examples of programme aims from UK universities

The aim of this ... degree is to provide you with the knowledge and skills needed to work in the modern digital media industry. It aims to provide you with a broad knowledge base across a range of convergent media types, including music and audio production, sound engineering, animation, television and web. The programme aims to provide you with both creative skills to generate and produce digital media content and the technical knowledge needed to deliver this content to an audience. (BSc (Hons) Professional Sound and Video Technology, University of Salford)

This study programme has been developed to respond to immense changes within the criminal justice system and society as a whole. These changes demand a new generation of criminal justice professionals who, in addition to understanding criminological issues, also understand the issues and complexities of living and working in a society containing a multiplicity of cultural and multicultural values. This degree aims to produce graduates to meet these needs. (BA (Hons) Criminology and Contemporary Culture, Manchester Metropolitan University)

This degree programme aims to produce engineers with a deep understanding of both hardware and software, able to lead the teams that design and build complete computerised systems. (BSc Electronic and Software Engineering, University of Glasgow)

Course outcomes

Whereas aims focus on what the course team wants to achieve, outcomes are about what students will be able to do. It is usual to structure learning outcomes by prefacing them by *On completion of the course participants will be able to...*; this leads naturally to an outcome which can be assessed. Figure 6.2 has some fictitious examples.

Figure 6.2 Examples of course outcomes

At the end of this programme, participants will be able to:

- present their work orally and in writing to a high standard

- analyse and evaluate relevant information to generate new perspectives on the subject

- solve problems autonomously in a range of professional situations

- work in a team to complete a project

- identify and analyse relationships between techniques and use these to develop new approaches in the laboratory

- treat patients compassionately with respect for their privacy and dignity

- respect client confidentiality

- work to a client's brief to produce a product which is fit for purpose and value for money

---

Course outcomes do not need to contain detail about curriculum content – that will appear in individual module outcomes – but they should relate to the discipline area and any professional skills which are essential. Quality Assurance Agency (QAA) qualification descriptors, including relevant subject benchmark statements as described in Chapter one, provide general guidance about what must be covered in the whole course. If the award is accredited by an external organisation, this body may also have a view on what needs to be included – sometimes they have precise requirements. The number of outcomes should ideally be limited to a number which the team can easily monitor and ensure that they are achieved by the combination of modules and assessment tasks being offered.

First thoughts about assessment

Once the course aims and outcomes have been written, the team can brainstorm their overall ideas for assessment. What kinds of assessments would show that students had achieved the course learning outcomes? Figure 6.3

shows some indicative assessment tasks for each of the sample learning outcomes in figure 6.2.

This gives the team an idea of what assessment to aim for when they write individual module specifications. At the end of the planning process the team can reconcile this list with the actual assessment tasks which have been devised for each module.

Figure 6.3 Sample course outcomes or objectives

At the end of this programme, participants will be able to:	Which might be tested by:
Present their work orally and in writing to a high standard	Individual presentations Group presentations Poster presentations Essays Dissertation Oral examination
Analyse and evaluate relevant information to generate new perspectives on the subject	Essay Dissertation Project report
Solve problems autonomously in a range of professional situations	Case Study Exam Role play Work placement report Portfolio
Work in a team to complete a project	Group case study Group organisation of an event
Identify and analyse relationships between techniques and use these to develop new approaches in the laboratory	Practical project report Practical examination
Treat patients compassionately with respect for their privacy and dignity	Work placement report Portfolio Practical examination
Respect client confidentiality	Work placement report Reflective analysis of a range of situations
Work to a client's brief to produce a product which is fit for purpose and value for money	Work placement report Product or exhibition Competition entry

Module aims

The aims for each individual module are usually succinct, summarising the module in a sentence or two. Module aims often appear in prospectuses and further course details. Examples are given in Figure 6.4.

Figure 6.4 Examples of module aims

This module aims to introduce students to the study of politics and explain the role and value of political discourse in modern society. (Level 4 Politics)

In this module, students will apply skills learned in previous levels to solve problems taken from real situations and compare them with the solutions actually adopted in practice (Level 6 Business Studies)

Module Learning Outcomes

For the individual lecturer, the most important parts of the module specification are the module learning outcomes and the assessment tasks. Traditionally, the list of content was considered to be the starting point of module design, but Part one of this book has shown that the availability of information, and the changes in the organisation of, and access to, higher education make higher education today more oriented to outcomes than induction into the privileged world of those with access to information. What is taught is still very important, but even more important now is that students are taught to identify, analyse and evaluate the sources of information available to them and to process, synthesise and present their findings appropriately.

Writing clear, assessable learning outcomes for individual modules is a skill. It should focus on what students will be able to *do* as a result of the unit. The content of the module becomes shaped by 'what students need to be told to help them to achieve the outcomes'.

Like course outcomes, module outcomes are most useful if they are conceptualised according to: what will students be able to do at the end of this module? A frequently used mnemonic for outcomes of any kind is *SMART*. There are a few variations on the interpretation of the last three letters, but all express what students could reasonably achieve in the time available and which can be assessed with reliability and validity. This one is common:

Specific, Measurable, Achievable, Relevant, Timely

Specificity

Module learning outcomes should be specific, unlike course outcomes, which encompass a large range of activities. The wording will depend on the subject area and the level of study. *Bloom's Taxonomy* (Bloom, 1956), or a variation of it (Anderson, 2001), are commonly used for categorising educational outcomes hierarchically. Using these taxonomies, modules which are designed for early parts of a course will focus more on knowledge, skills and basic applications, whereas final year undergraduates and postgraduates will be expected to analyse and evaluate what they find and even create new approaches, products or perspectives. To help with writing learning outcomes, many useful lists of action verbs have already been compiled. Figure 6.5 gives some examples.

Figure 6.5 some useful verbs to use in learning outcomes, using Anderson and Krathwohl's (2001) revised taxonomy for classification. This is a short, simplified list but it illustrates the notion of progression:

1. Remembering: describe, label, recall, recognise, retrieve

2. Understanding: classify, explain, summarise

3. Applying: apply, choose, illustrate, model, plan, select, solve, use

4. Analysing: analyse, compare, contrast, debate, distinguish, organise, simplify

5. Evaluating: check, critique, evaluate, measure

6. Creating: create, generate, plan, predict, produce, propose, revise

---

Verbs such as 'know' or 'understand' should be avoided because they are difficult to assess. If a learning outcome says that that students should *Know about the composition of the UK and Irish Parliaments*, how could they demonstrate this? Would writing a list of the important features of the two systems be sufficient? If the learning outcome said instead *compare the composition of the UK and Irish Parliaments with reference to their effectiveness in passing legislation*, it is clear that students are expected to analyse and evaluate what happens in each situation.

This example demonstrates the importance of **context** in the learning outcomes. A school student of politics might be expected to list the important features of the two parliamentary systems, and maybe compare the differences. A foundation degree student might be expected to obtain the information to make a judgement on effectiveness, whilst an under-graduate would be expected to analyse and make a judgement on effectiveness. A post-graduate could design a new system based on the best of both. Well written learning outcomes will make such context clear.

Context also depends on the discipline. An outcome like *analyse the properties of Perspex* has different meanings to a physicist, a chemist and an environmental scientist. The addition of *mechanical, chemical* or *environmental impact* before the word *properties* would indicate differences in what is actually done on the module and the final assessment tasks.

Measurability

The success of the student in achieving the learning outcome needs to be measurable. Refining the learning outcomes and the assessment tasks form an iterative process in which the outcomes are drafted, the assessment is considered, then checked against the outcomes. For the first draft of the outcomes, a rough idea is sufficient. We look at assessment task design in the next section.

Achievability

Learning outcomes have to be realistic in scope. Taking a simplistic example, a student beginning a new language is unlikely to be able to translate a scholarly work at the end of 200 hours of study. There needs to be a sense of where students are at the start of the module as well as where they should be at the end. As we discussed in Part One, this can be difficult, because students come from diverse educational and cultural backgrounds and assumptions can be incorrect. But some guesses will be needed in order to plan the module effectively. During the lifetime of the course, these suppositions should be revisited and may lead to modification of the learning outcomes if needed.

Relevance

The relevance of learning outcomes should be cross-referenced to the course aims and outcomes. To what extent does this module contribute to one or more of them? How well does it fit in? If it does not, but the importance of the module is agreed, then the course aims and outcomes may need to be modified.

Timeliness

It must be possible for a student to achieve the learning outcomes in the time allocated for the module and for assessment tasks to be set at appropriate times during the module. The number of student learning hours assigned to the module is clearly important, but so is the format, as considered below. The learning outcomes may need to be fine-tuned again once this is decided.

Designing assessment tasks

Once a set of learning outcomes has been determined, the next step is to design the assessment strategy which tests whether or not the outcomes have been achieved.

John Biggs coined the expression 'constructive alignment' to describe the relationship between learning outcomes and assessment (Biggs, 2003; Biggs and Tang, 2007). He maintained that the intended learning outcomes should provide a framework for all aspects of the teaching of a particular module. The constructive alignment approach acknowledges the assessment-centred focus more naturally adopted by time-starved students, rather than the curriculum content-centred approach traditionally used by academic staff in course planning. If teaching and learning activities are planned around the assessment tasks for the module, it is clearly in the students' interests to attend sessions and complete formative learning activities during the module.

The argument against being assessment-focused in curriculum planning is the possible loss of the joys of serendipitous learning. This can be countered by providing plenty of opportunities for autonomous learning, problem-solving and asking open-ended questions. There are competing pressures on curriculum design in higher education, but it should still aim to help students develop as rounded individuals. Learning outcomes which encourage comparison, contrast and reflection enable students to learn creatively whilst still working towards the assessment tasks which have been set.

Figure 6.6 opposite shows an example of using constructive alignment to work out an assessment strategy. The documentation to be provided is all in the form of written materials; the difference between this assessment task and a traditional essay submission is that the participant is asked to develop something work-related which they will defend to their peers, and then provide a critical reflection of the processes they used and the outcomes of the task. The learning outcomes are being assessed but each submission will inevitably be different, because it is linked to each student's personal work situation. It isn't always possible to personalise tasks to the experience of the individual in this way, but it certainly makes plagiarism more difficult when each individual's task is slightly different. It also makes the assignments more interesting to mark.

Figure 6.6 Example of assessment strategy linked to module learning outcomes

Module Learning outcomes On completion of this unit participants will be able to:	Assessment strategy
1. Prepare an academic rationale for a curriculum development proposal	A. The completion of a programme unit proposal for 'minor modification' based on relevant sections of current university documentation which will be assessed by a panel of peers (role play situation) Participants are encouraged to use 'real-life' proposals from their own discipline. (assessing learning outcomes 1-3) (approximately 1000 words).
2. Devise appropriate Learning Outcomes and a strategy for their assessment	
3. Construct a curriculum proposal that addresses the academic standards and quality precepts of institutional procedures and QAA's Academic Infrastructure	
4. Critically evaluate programme documentation for purposes of approval or review	B. A written critique of the Self-evaluation document provided for a case study role play (approximately 1000 words). C. A critical analysis of the effectiveness of the panel's deliberations in a case study role play (approximately 1000 words). (assessing learning outcome 4)

Use a simple two column grid like the one in figure 6.6 to compare the learning outcomes and the assessment tasks to check that they are fully aligned. It is surprising how often there is a learning outcome which doesn't seem to be directly assessed, or something being assessed which is not expressed as an intended learning outcome. Assessment tasks may need to be innovative to cover all the outcomes. This kind of grid also helps determine whether the result of an activity is being assessed, or the process by which that result was achieved, or both. For instance, is the content alone of an oral presentation being assessed, or is the way in which it is presented important as well?

As the previous section indicated, it is likely that the assessment strategy and learning outcomes will be developed as an iterative process and they will both need adjustment until they are properly aligned.

Innovation in assessment

Academics have a good deal of autonomy when selecting assessment tasks for students. Yet although people who work in higher education are reflective and innovative, tradition still guides assessment design. Students in humanities still write a lot of essays; students in art and design still present their work formally to their peers for critique; science students still write laboratory reports. Unseen exams at the end of the course often still count for a large share of the marks.

In the first decade of the 21st century there were some changes in the pattern of assessments, but a student from the 1960s would usually recognise the assessments in their subject area today. Many would argue that this is a good thing: it shows that there are some consistent values, and we can compare this year's alumni with the past. Some people see different forms of assessment task as evidence of dumbing down in the educational system – that we are trying too hard to accommodate students who would not have been up to it in the past.

Such views are fairly widespread and those who would like to introduce novel methods of assessment can find them difficult to challenge. It can be argued that the profile of students in HE has changed in the last twenty years and that some of the purposes of HE are different today, so assessment tasks should accommodate these changes.

Students who have different skills and backgrounds need to be given opportunities to show their ability to fulfil learning outcomes at a higher level. People who are dyslexic, for example, rarely managed to complete degrees in any subject except art and design in the past, because most other courses relied on essays and unseen exams requiring short essays. Only writing could demonstrate their reasoning skills and knowledge, so their disability effectively excluded them from sections of higher education. We now have a broader range of definitions of what it means to be *up to it* in higher education and our assessment strategies should reflect this.

The purposes of HE are also now broader and more varied. Many forms of professional training that would have been work-based in the past now require graduate status. Some see this as a political decision, but it can also be viewed as being about ensuring that professionals such as nurses, teachers, accountants and engineers have graduate-level skills of expression, analysis, synthesis and reflection in addition to the required professional skills. Assessment tasks need to reflect these purposes and relate them to professional contexts.

One reason for using conventional assessment tasks is the understandable wish to feel comfortable with the familiar. Assessment is the only way for students to show their achievement, and experimenting with it can cause unease. External examiners, examination board chairs, assessment administrators, professional body representatives are all familiar with essays and exams. Something new can only be implemented if it is fully understood. A clear plan is needed for the whole process: distributing the task to students and giving them support, submission rules, assessment criteria, marking, feedback, moderating and arrangements for resits. Trying something out as a formative assessment first can be useful.

Curriculum content

What needs to be taught so that students can achieve the assessment? In almost all subjects there is a core canon, particularly for early under-graduate work, which all graduates are expected to know about or be able to do.

For a final year or post-graduate subject in a specialised area, it may be possible to start from scratch with the content for a brand new module. If so, think about what the students might know when they start, and the additional content they need in order to achieve the module learning outcomes. Knowing what they have done before on the programme and how this new module follows on is as critical as ensuring continuity within modules.

Curriculum design is more likely to be associated with reviewing a module which has already been offered, or adapting an existing module for a new purpose. The existing material is a good starting point, but once the learning outcomes and assessment tasks have been updated, changes might be needed to the existing content. It is advisable to discuss this with colleagues who have taught this or a similar module. Would the proposed changes help or hinder students in completing the module successfully, or cause problems later in the course?

For first year (level 4) courses, examples of A-level and Diploma syllabuses give an idea of what students have done previously, even though not all students will have followed these programmes or used the same exam board. Likewise, any feeder foundation or access course will indicate what has already been covered.

Looking at what is taught in other institutions which offer the same subject is also useful. Curriculum details can be checked on the internet, or other departments contacted to see what they do in individual modules and offering to share completed proposals in return. Even if institutions compete for students, many people will be happy to share this kind of information. Higher Education Academy subject centres are particularly useful, both for curriculum ideas and for examples of how to incorporate topics and try out different activities. They generally have resources such as surveys of skill development needs in the subject area, and can answer questions about selection of content or recommend colleagues from the subject area who are willing to compare notes.

What matters when deciding on module content is what students need to know in order to achieve the learning outcomes. There will be interesting or extending items for them to know, but the learning outcomes must determine the content.

When there is a rough list of content, decisions must be made about how much time students would need to spend on each topic to achieve the level expected. Most institutions work to an approximate student workload figure of 10 hours of total student effort for 1 credit point. Total student effort includes taught sessions as well as private study time. After allowing for the assignment task – probably at least 25 per cent of the module time – there may be too little or, more likely, too much content for the allotted hours. It is better to try to cover less content in more depth than more content superficially, because studying one topic in depth prepares students better for finding out about other topics in the future. However for some subjects a certain number of topics *must* be studied. If the number of credit points allocated to a module seems too restricting, it might be possible to negotiate with the rest of the course team for more time, or suggest that some of the content is delivered in another module.

Learning and Teaching Activities

Rather than a plan of the whole unit in programme documentation or at an approval or review event, a rough plan will suffice for questions to be answered confidently.

Figure 6.7 opposite gives an example plan for the post-graduate module shown in figure 6.6. The activities are indicative, but show how the work might be divided up.

Figure 6.7: Example of linking learning and teaching activities to assessment tasks (100 hours student effort)

Learning outcomes	Assessment tasks	Possible learning and teaching activities
1. Prepare an academic rationale for a curriculum development proposal	A. The completion of a programme unit proposal for 'minor modification' based on relevant sections of current university documentation which will be assessed by a panel of peers (role play situation) Participants are encouraged to use 'real-life' proposals from their own discipline (assessing learning outcomes 1-3) (approximately 1000 words)	Review exemplar academic rationales: mini-lecture plus workshop activity. Private study reviewing existing rationales (one given by tutor, one from own course) (total 10 hours)
2. Devise appropriate Learning Outcomes and a strategy for their assessment		Writing sample outcomes – peer review: submission to VLE of sample outcomes then each participant reviews outcomes provided by two other participants (total 10 hours)
		Classroom review of VLE activity, then review and evaluate existing assessment strategies: mini-lecture plus workshop activity. Private study reviewing theory and evidence-base, then reviewing own course strategy (total 25 hours)
3. Construct a curriculum proposal that addresses the academic standards and quality precepts of institutional procedures and QAA's Academic Infrastructure		Search for and review available curriculum information – Professional bodies, HEA subject centres, Regional development agencies, benchmarking with other institutions Know about QAA benchmarks and code of practice

Figure 6.7: Example of linking learning and teaching activities to assessment tasks (100 hours student effort) (continued)

Learning outcomes	Assessment tasks	Possible learning and teaching activities
		Lecture plus formative in-class test plus private study (total 10 hours)
		Role-play review event – produce and present documentation to panel (composed of peers plus two experienced panel members)
		Serve on role-play panel. Private study review activity of panel and process of documentation production. (total 40 hours)
4. Critically evaluate programme documentation for purposes of approval or review	B. A written critique of the Self-evaluation document provided for a case study role play (approximately 1000 words) C. A critical analysis of the effectiveness of the panel's deliberations in a case study role play (approximately 1000 words) (assessing learning outcome 4)	Develop and agree criteria for successful documentation – in class workshop (total 5 hours)

Module organisation

Once the aims, objectives and outline content of a module are determined, think about how it will be delivered and the range of techniques to use. In most institutions, teaching sessions are evenly distributed across the teaching year or semester (one lecture per week per module, for instance) so that students have some teaching from each of their modules every week. This is the long and thin approach, as opposed to short and fat, in which modules are completed in shorter blocks. On the long thin model, full-time students might work simultaneously on six 20 credit modules across the academic year, whereas on a short fat model, they might study two modules at a time in three blocks of eight teaching weeks each. Part-time students may require a completely different approach.

Long thin modules allow students to spend time reading widely and developing original ideas and their own approaches to the topic, as well as developing skills of analysis, reflection and synthesis – all essential elements of higher education. However, other types of skills are better developed in a more intensive format. All disciplines have some tools of the trade which need to be mastered quickly: laboratory techniques in science, use of specialised equipment in art and design or engineering, classroom organisation in education, précis writing in the humanities, legal report writing in law, and so on. These kinds of topics, where students are expected to learn new skills, generally work better in short fat mode, giving students opportunities to practice, review and retry without forgetting their errors and successes between sessions. It is equivalent to an intensive driving or swimming course – ideal for the skills in which they need to become so proficient that they don't have to think about the basic techniques each time they apply themselves to more advanced situations.

In practice, module organisation is something of a compromise. Timetabling is a complex business in large institutions, and individual influence over the process is limited, especially if something unfamilar to the institution is being suggested. However, even if the timetable cannot be reorganised completely, teaching slots might be exchanged between colleagues so that module A gets more slots early in the term by taking some of the module B slots, and the reverse later on in the term. This would allow for a more intensive induction period so that students can practice and become proficient in core skills early on in their courses.

The timetable may seem to define teaching techniques. Custom and practice or considerations of space will mean that large numbers of students are timetabled to attend at certain times and smaller groups at others. The timetable might look rigid, but we saw in Chapter four that lectures or seminars could cover a wide range of teaching techniques, and these can vary during the year. Students generally shift from dependence on the tutor at first to independent capability. Students may be closely directed early in the module, then guided in structured work towards working independently on a final assignment which achieves all the module learning outcomes. Students develop through their years of study: foundation degree students may not achieve autonomy but masters level students should be working independently in specialised areas.

Assessment Criteria

Assessment criteria are used to judge the standard achieved in each learning outcome. Some are specific to the assignment but generic marking criteria are generally developed for the course. This approach has advantages over having individual assessment criteria for each assignment. Firstly, generic criteria should help students understand how judgements are being made throughout the course and, secondly, the same feedback forms can be used for every assignment, allowing students and personal tutors to identify strengths and areas for development. However, individual module criteria may be more effective in certain situations.

At both module or course level, assessment criteria are written by the course team so that any differences of interpretation can be discussed as they are written. The whole team needs to be clear about the meaning of commonly used words in assessment regulations such as *threshold, good* and *excellent*. Universities in the UK usually require percentage grades, which are linked to grade descriptors such as fail, bare fail, pass, good, very good, excellent, mapped in turn onto the standard UK degree classification system of pass, third, 2(ii), 2(i), first. Countries such as India and Australia use a similar system, while the USA uses the letters A – F, and France has a system of marks out of 20.

Whatever the system, course teams should discuss what a student would need to be able to do to achieve the learning outcomes at threshold level, what the best achievements would be like, and then work out what kind of work might fall in between. The institution's assessment policy should offer guidance about grading.

External examiners' reports often comment that course teams rarely use the full range of marks available. This is particularly true at the high end. Examination boards often see marks clustered around 70 per cent, making it difficult even for the most able students to achieve a first class degree. If the 70 per cent-100 per cent category which indicates a first class mark in most UK institutions is divided into 'excellent' and 'outstanding', it is easier to identify work which deserves the very highest marks.

There should be clear linkage between programme (or unit) learning outcomes, assessment strategies (how outcomes are expected to be demonstrated) and assessment criteria (how different levels of achievement of those outcomes are distinguished and recognised). It is important that the programme team and students have a shared understanding, so there is consistency in marking and a mark is clearly justified. When marking criteria are fully understood, the full marking scale is more likely to be used, with less of the typical cautious bunching between 50 and 68 per cent (Yorke, Bridges *et al*, 2000) – feedback should closely align personal comments with the numerical mark.

Feedback policy

Giving feedback on assessed work, discussed in Chapter five, is easily done in the context of a well planned feedback strategy which links to the assessment planning. Planning for marking and feedback at the same time as making a teaching plan makes life easier, but how many of us do it as routine? It is tempting not to think about marking and feedback until the evil hour arrives. It is rarely a requirement of a university's quality systems to include a feedback policy in the substantial programme documentation. But planning it in advance of teaching the module makes it easier to give students useful feedback.

A good feedback policy starts with key aims. The Quality Assurance Agency (QAA) code of practice for the assurance of academic quality and standards in higher education states that 'Institutions [should] provide appropriate and timely feedback to students on assessed work in a way that promotes learning and facilitates improvement but does not increase the burden of assessment' (QAA, 2006).

According to Nicol and Macfarlane (2006), good feedback practice

1. helps clarify what good performance is (goals, criteria, expected standards)
2. facilitates the development of self-assessment (reflection) in learning
3. delivers high quality information to students about their learning
4. encourages teacher and peer dialogue around learning
5. encourages positive motivational beliefs and self-esteem
6. provides opportunities to close the gap between current and desired performance
7. provides information to teachers that can be used to help shape teaching.

Having a formal policy helps explain the approach to colleagues and students, check processes more systematically and introduce changes which fit in with the policy. It should also reduce the apparently insatiable demands of marking and feedback by setting clear limits for what will be done and relating it clearly to student outcomes. The goal is a policy which enables module co-

---

Figure 6.8: Sample module feedback statement

The assignment for this module must be submitted on the dates indicated in the unit hand-book. I will provide feedback within four weeks of this date. My individual feedback to you will consist of

1. a mark

2. a copy of the assessment criteria grid (see programme handbook) with highlighting to show where you have achieved the different criteria

3. an indication of which parts of the assignment you carried out well

4. an indication of where there is room for improvement together with individual sugges-tions for how to do this if appropriate

In most cases this individual feedback will be brief and I will also provide generic feedback to the whole group during our session in week 20, which will go through some common suc-cesses and areas for development on the assignment. I will discuss individual assignments during my regular office hours on condition that you have reflected carefully on the feedback, both individual and generic, in relation to your own work.

---

ordinators to produce a feedback statement for each module which supports the programme aims, such as the sample statement shown in Figure 6.8.

Students need to know to what degree they have achieved the unit learning outcomes, and what they should concentrate on in future assignments. The feedback should enable the students to learn from what they have done and from the assessment of it.

Phil Race suggests that feedback is better thought of as 'feed forward' (Race, 2005) and should contain:

- details of what would have been necessary to get a higher grade
- suggestions for things to try in the next assignment
- suggestions about sources

A policy should indicate what kinds of areas will generate feedback for each assignment. This may lead naturally from existing assessment criteria or these might need revising. For example, if learning outcomes and assessment criteria for a unit or programme don't cover transferable skills such as writing or oral presentation, and the team thinks that these are important, the out-comes and criteria may need to be revisited. If students need specific help with, for instance, spelling, grammar or structuring work, the feedback should indicate where this is available.

The World of Work

Higher education is a short stage in most people's lives, after which they do other things. So their education should help prepare them for what comes next. This book emphasises the need to think about where students have come from; it is also important to think about where they might be going once they leave higher education. For vocational courses such as medicine, teaching, nursing, physiotherapy, law or accountancy, this may be fairly straightforward, even if students have a wide choice of specialism once they begin their professional lives. In non-vocational subjects, the future careers available to graduates may be more varied but previous experience of graduate destinations from the subject will give some clues. Activities that allow students to develop abilities which will be useful in a wide range of professional situations can be built into the curriculum. Some programme teams do this by creating special employability modules which enable students to provide evidence of academic achievement linked to activities outside the classroom, whilst others integrate these activities into one or more of the subject-based modules.

Generic skills relating to presentation and communication skills, retrieving and analysing information, working in teams, problem solving and so on are likely to be identified in the programme aims and outcomes. These skills will be assessed as part of the assessment strategy for the course, but it may also be possible to identify situations where students can be given a richer experience of the relevance of their studies to the world of work.

Work placements

Work placements are often a compulsory element of vocational courses, ensuring that students are assessed in a realistic professional situation. They may also be offered as an option, so that students spend a summer, or the third year of a four year course, in employment linked to their course. Such placements are thought to increase students' employability and are popular with employers (Bennett *et al*, 2008) and can help students to make links between academic study and future employment.

The identification and organisation of work placements is a significant undertaking for a course team. Departments or schools, or the university as a whole, may have an administrative infrastructure in place to support this, but resourcing such activity may be difficult if this is not the case. Others may need to be convinced that this is worthwhile activity in the subject area. Building support for work placements in the department might be achieved by integrating assessments linked to voluntary work or simulated work situations, or by seeing if links can be made with a social enterprise in the region.

Small grants may be available to research and pilot interesting and innovative ideas for work placements in particular subject areas.

Most UK institutions will have an Institutional Code of Practice for work placements, as recommended by the QAA, which will specify the documentation which needs to be prepared. Colleagues from other courses in the institution which have work placements may be prepared to explain the institution's regulations and processes, share copies of the documentation needed for students, placement providers and supervising tutors, and outline the resource needs.

Compulsory work placements may take the form of a year out of formal study working in a company, or, if integrated into courses such as teaching or health care, last from 6-12 weeks during the academic year or the summer. Universities usually organise placements via direct contact with employers and workplaces. Making these contacts, keeping up to date information about the numbers of students who could be placed and the possible dates they can be accepted, and monitoring students out on placement can be quite time-consuming.

There are several ways of assessing student performance on work placements. Portfolios can record what was done and the students' reflections on it to show their development as reflective professionals; reports from the employer together with a reflective summary of what the student has learned show whether they were able to carry out realistic work projects and link them to their studies; students could give a presentation on the company and its core business; or students could write an account of what it is like to work in a multidisciplinary team.

Optional work placements may be an attractive selling point for a course as long as there are resources to support finding them and linking them into the curriculum. Such placements usually take place during the vacation and are seldom monitored formally, although techniques suggested for accrediting unstructured learning opportunities (Chapter five) could be used to give students credit for optional placements.

Voluntary work

Voluntary work is an underused way of linking academic work to practical applications. Many Students' Unions organise community and voluntary work and should be able to provide practical advice for setting up links. Links they have already developed such as working with the community (legal advice centres, sports coaching, working with the elderly, school exclusion programmes, etc) may connect directly to some courses, but for others thought may need to be given to the skills they would develop in students. Organising a team to clear a section of riverbank, for instance, would require planning, communication and team management skills and health and safety knowledge, which might all be useful in the future. History students could volunteer to do secondary research for a local history society. Language students could offer translation and interpretation services for the local community. Many such activities go on already – could they be linked to module learning outcomes so that students can include their experiences in their assessed work? If work placements are optional, a choice of assignment tasks would need to be offered, some of which did not depend on a placement.

Social enterprises

Social enterprises are businesses which can make a profit but also aim to meet a social need. Such enterprises often offer students opportunities for voluntary or paid work placements like those mentioned above. Some universities have set up such companies themselves with the dual aim of giving their students relevant work experiences whilst providing a service to the community. As well as translation services, web page design, event management, tour guiding, family history research, art classes, sports coaching and archiving services, there are many more possibilities. There might be sources of internal support for a pilot scheme, or the local council may have pump-priming funds, or an HEA subject centre could have funding for a small project.

Case studies and simulations for employability

There is nothing new about including realistic case studies and simulations in the curriculum (see Chapter five). Science students do laboratory work, engineers make prototypes, business students study company documentation and art students work to briefs. Other subject areas may require creative thinking along the lines of the suggestions in Figure 6.8 (overleaf).

Evaluation of Higher Education

Publicly funded services are under increasing scrutiny from users and funding bodies. Potential students and their parents want to be able to make quantitative and qualitative comparisons of courses; funders of research want to know where the best quality research will be obtained; the government wants to ensure value for money. In addition, professionals wish to improve their own practice and so need to know whether their aims are being achieved. In order to meet all of these expectations, institutions of HE are subject to a good deal of measurement and inspection.

Figure 6.8 Suggestions for incorporating employability activities into teaching

■ Find a newspaper article which purports to reference the subject but is misleading. Students could rewrite the article accurately, or do an analysis of the article which shows its fallacies and misinterpretations

■ Encourage students to think creatively about links between the subject and the wider world: ask them to work as a team to produce a three minute video which explains the relevance to the community of what they are studying, or make a proposal for a social enterprise which uses what they have learned, or develop a study guide for new entrants to the subject

■ Bring in a speaker to talk about what they learned from studying the subject and how they use it now. This is a stimulus for debate and reporting on topics such as 'key skills I will need to develop' or 'what kinds of activities would help me to get to the same position as that speaker?', or even 'what I would do differently from that speaker?'

In the UK, research has been subject since 1986 to evaluation of this kind. The Research Assessment Exercise used measures such as number of papers published and value of research contracts to rate individual researchers and subject teams. The outcomes of the assessment are used to determine the distribution of HEFCE research funding, so are taken extremely seriously by institutions, and much time goes into ensuring that the relevant data is available and robust. Research evaluation is being developed under the title of Research Excellence Framework (see Chapter one), to take greater account of the impact that research has on society.

Institutions conduct their own formal and informal evaluations of teaching, but following the Dearing Review (NCIHE, 1997) (see Chapter one), the UK has developed national approaches to collecting information about teaching performance and the student experience. It has proved difficult to develop really robust methods for judging the quality of teaching and learning, so a variety of sources is generally used: student evaluations, statistics about institutions and monitoring of processes. Statistics for individual courses drawn from these sources are now gathered together on a website, Unistats.co.uk, to help potential students choose suitable courses. Newspapers also use the data, weighted according to their views of the relative importance of the various factors, to construct league tables of institutions and subject areas, so they are very important for the overall reputation of the institution as well as for informing prospective students.

In addition to public compilation of data, institutions collect private information to help them assess quality, such as the number of academic appeals and plagiarism cases, how many academic staff engage in staff development activity, student perceptions of individual modules, how well the library works, whether students think there are enough computers, if the chips in the canteen are tasty, and so on. Institutions are groaning under the weight of such evaluation data.

The scrutiny associated with evaluation can seem like an unwelcome burden at times. But practitioners need to see it positively: it enables potential students to make informed decisions about their studies from the increasingly diverse sector and a general desire to get value for money. The next section looks at how people working in these institutions can use information to improve student experience and think how they might contribute to quality assurance and quality enhancement.

Course Approval and Review

As part of their compliance with the QAA code of practice (see Chapter one), institutions have course approval and review processes which ensure that courses fit into the agreed structures and meet minimum requirements for documentation. Approval processes need to be completed before a course can begin, and periodic review is usually carried out every five or six years or more frequently if issues have been identified or if an external validating organisation works to a different timetable. External validating organisations called Professional, Regulatory and Statutory Bodies (PSRBs) usually offer professional accreditation or exemptions on top of academic qualifications. Examples are the Solicitors Regulation Authority, the Nursing and Midwifery Council, the Engineering Council or the Institute of Chartered Accountants.

Periodic reviews will take into account much of the publicly available data about the course and invite tutors, students and other interested parties such as employers or PSRBs to give their views on how things are going. Most university employees are involved in approval and review at some time in their careers, as these activities permeate all elements of university life. People may be called upon to prepare documentation, design elements of the curriculum, support resource allocations, analyse performance data, or sit on panels. It is worth finding out how the processes work and who is responsible for which aspects of them. Like most specialist areas, quality assurance and quality enhancement has its own jargon but decoding acronyms will improve engagement with the processes and link them more closely to the development of learning, teaching and assessment.

Publicly available data
National Student Survey

The National Student Survey (NSS), similar to the Course Experience Survey in Australia, asks final year students about their overall satisfaction with their programmes, including the teaching and assessment. Funded by HEFCE since 2005 and carried out by an independent survey organisation, it generates an enormous quantity of data and provides an overall picture of the student experience in a subject area. The data is also used as a factor in certain newspaper league table rankings based on the average institutional results, so it is intensely interesting for university governing bodies and councils.

NSS data can be used to point to areas of development and further investigation. It paints a broad picture of the student experience but lacks the detail for an action plan for improvement. The performances of different subject areas in the NSS vary widely, so it is seldom useful to use the data to compare different subjects in the same institution, although it can be useful to compare data for a department or programme with those of counterparts elsewhere.

In addition to the publicly available summary of responses to 22 multiple choice questions, institutions receive copies of students' responses to open questions asking them to indicate the most positive and negative aspects of their courses. These open responses help provide clues to the responses to the multiple choice questions and often highlight the issues which were pre-occupying students.

Higher Education Statistics Agency

The government set up the Higher Education Statistics Agency (HESA) in 1993 to collect quantitative data from institutions, such as figures for graduate employment, retention rates, staff-student ratios, the number of students who get a 'good' degree, spend per student and so on. These statistics are available in various formats to different audiences, and can be used for comparative purposes.

Course Data
Module evaluation

Information about individual modules usually comes from a variety of sources: end of unit evaluation, student representation at committees, external examiners' reports, informal conversations with students, student performance levels, student attendance levels and tutor reflections. When combined, they give a picture of the overall performance of the unit and what kinds of enhancement may be needed. The collection of data under each heading may vary, but every institution aims for high levels of student satisfaction and a profile of student performance which seems to reflect expectations of the cohort. Information from module evaluation is used to inform enhancement of modules and courses, and also feeds into institutional evaluations and reviews.

Because modules are usually taught and managed by individuals or small teams, people may feel sensitive about evaluations of this kind. Arthur (2009) analysed the responses of academic staff to student evaluation and classified them into four categories (figure 6.9) which may seem familiar. People who can reframe what they do with students in a positive way will enhance their work constructively.

This task should be approached without the 'blame' or 'shame' as identified by Arthur. Nobody teaches perfectly all the time; no modules remain the same for long; nobody ever has the ideal teaching environment. Any experienced, popular lecturer will admit that they sometimes have bad days in the classroom: what makes them effective teachers is their ability to learn from those experiences and change their practices accordingly. They can also discard outlying data from their review such as one really bad, spiteful evaluation or a student who failed because of external circumstances. There will be

---

Figure 6.9: responses to student evaluation – after Arthur (2009)

	Lecturer feels able to influence	
Tame: I can respond to their needs and bring them on board		Reframe: It's to do with me, but I can learn and develop
Factors relate to students		Factors relate to lecturers
Blame: it's their fault and I can't do anything about it		Shame: it's my fault and I can't do anything about it
	Lecturer feels unable to influence	

---

some things that can be developed as a small team, or individually if necessary, without having to make significant changes to timetabling or curriculum approval. Thinking about and developing teaching style, attitudes to students and approaches to collaboration with colleagues can also help.

It is very tempting just to focus on the negative aspects of student evaluation: in our experience 99 per cent of students may love the course but we tend only to see and remember the views of the 1 per cent who do not. But students may also highlight effective innovative practice that can be shared with colleagues. Aiming to situate the response in the 'reframing' quadrant of Arthur's diagram will help to keep a sense of perspective.

Quick wins

If there is a need for change, starting with something small can give a quick win. It demonstrates willingness to respond to feedback and helps build confidence. For example:

- If students said that some lectures are boring, use one new technique, review it, consolidate it in a second session, and try another technique in a third session. Vary the way a lecture starts or ends, or add a video clip, or introduce a new activity half way through. This doesn't take long to prepare or evaluate, and techniques can be added over time.

- Students might ask for theoretical lectures to have more grounding with practical examples so they seem more relevant. Are there any techniques which could be used to relate theory to real life? (see chapter five).

- If students seem to be underperforming, or say they are having difficulty understanding, then try to explain in a variety of ways – use diagrams, video clips, sound effects or demonstrations. Ask students about where they get lost – the 'one minute paper' technique described in Chapter four can be used for anonymous feedback. This is quick and easy to process, even for a large group, and may offer clues as to the difficulties

- If there is a delay before students receive feedback, give the class generic feedback about their common strengths and weaknesses as soon as a few assignments have been marked. Discuss the processes of marking and moderation, and why this takes time.

- If evaluations are disappointing but the reasons for them aren't clear, try teaming up with a trusted colleague to share teaching and assessment on both modules. Team teaching provides peer support and new ideas for teaching, and it can be fun.

■ If students are asking for particular things, such as podcasts or more use of the VLE, look for a workshop on new techniques. If the institution doesn't offer anything, suggest that they do, or check the professional body or HEA subject centre, as many do provide workshops and mini-conferences on pedagogical issues.

Institutional enhancement

Module and course evaluations might reveal issues which are beyond individual control, such as organisation of timetables, timing of assessment points, library opening hours or access to equipment. In these circumstances, the information should be passed on to the relevant people in the institution. There is usually a system of annual monitoring which enables this to take place: issues are flagged in course reports, which are then integrated into departmental or faculty reports. These are then considered by the body which oversees academic standards, usually Senate or Academic Board. For anything that requires urgent attention the head of department or equivalent should be informed at once, but most issues will be resolved in the annual monitoring process where courses can be compared and patterns can be identified.

A picture of what is happening across all faculties or schools can be compiled from the publicly available data, information gathered from course and module evaluations, external examiners' reports, outcomes of course approval and review activities, and occasional surveys which focus on particular areas. Individual services of the university may carry out general improvements, or course teams may be asked to focus on particular areas such as the provision of feedback, or implementation of a VLE, and produce an action plan for development. Those who have expertise in one of these areas may be asked to support general institutional enhancement activity by serving on a working group, or by sharing good practice so that others can implement a particular technique.

Summary

Designing modules and assessment is a huge responsibility but also a great privilege and very satisfying. The sometimes competing demands of public accountability, disciplinary traditions and responsiveness to students can make the process challenging but we hope that the structured approach presented here will build confidence in taking the decisions necessary for effective curriculum design.

Conclusion
Next steps

This overview of the role of the academic in the 21st century university indicates the flexibility required to cope with a rapidly changing environment and focuses mainly on the day to day tasks. It concludes with a discussion about how an individual can manage their current and future roles in higher education.

Managing the present and the future

Being an academic requires people to take personal responsibility for managing their own time and prioritising tasks. The teaching timetable imposes a certain structure on the week and academic year; the parts of the job which fall outside this are both varied and variable. To meet the commitments decided for the year, academics need to manage their own time and priorities.

Autonomy is a major attraction of being an academic: it gives an important sense of being trusted to get on with the job. In a perfect world, it should make it easier to balance the manic moments of the academic calendar with the quieter ones: attending a school nativity play in the afternoon or being able to take a long weekend in the summer is paid for by the additional hours spent marking a hundred exam scripts within three days in May. Having access to the top people and resources in the field can be set against working all night in the laboratory to finish an experiment. Few other professional jobs allow people to work at home for a day to get some quiet thinking time, or indeed value thinking time in the same way.

The changes in higher education, as described in this book, have increased the diversity of opportunities available for workers in HE, but they add to the pressure to achieve across a range of domains: teaching, administration, research, enterprise, student support and so on. People can feel overwhelmed by what is asked of them but it's important to stay in control. Think how long the situation is likely to last. How much is in the person's control and how much seems to be because of what other people are demanding? Who can be approached about the situation? We have found it invaluable to have a trusted colleague who understands the strains and can help keep a sense of perspective and a sense of humour, whereas friends and family can find it difficult to understand the peaks and troughs of the job. Colleagues from other departments are particularly helpful, as their ups and downs are unlikely to coincide exactly with yours. Many institutions will find a mentor for a new member of staff and this can be especially valuable when they feel under pressure.

Working in HE is demanding, and the motivation that drew us into the profession can lead us to try to do too much. The job requires skills of personal interaction and making decisions which affect individuals, so personal well-being and morale are extremely important for us to be able to support our students.

Remembering why we were attracted to the job in the first place can counter frustrations. The desire to teach, support students, or do research may fade over time and need rekindling. Remembering positive experiences helps: that moment when a particular technique finally clicked for a student, or the day an experiment turned up unexpected results, or the conference presentation which was warmly praised by a respected colleague, or hearing that a committee had approved a proposed improvement to student support.

What comes next?

The conventional picture of a university lecturer is of somebody who combines teaching, research and related administration. A traditional career trajectory consisted of getting a PhD, then a research assistant (post-doc) position, then a lectureship. For those able to do enough good quality research, a personal chair in their research subject was considered the pinnacle of academic achievement. In many universities, the professors rotated the post of head of department every three years or so and then returned to their full-time research responsibilities. In others, the role of head of department was a permanent post which some academics sought. Senior managers almost always had an academic background.

Modern academic careers are much more complex. Whilst the research route to a personal chair might still be the gold standard for many, there are other opportunities to develop expertise and progress through the university structures. To the traditional mix of teaching, research and academic administration we can add 'enterprise' and other work which blurs the boundaries, such as research-informed teaching, liaison with regulatory bodies and organising work placements for students. In addition to the personal research chair, many institutions offer chairs for excellence in teaching or for work with external bodies, although research-type evidence of achievement, such as publications and peer esteem, is still needed.

Career paths are much more diverse, and administrative staff may also teach, carry out research and hold senior management posts such as head of department, head of services or registry, or Pro Vice-Chancellor.

No one is likely to do everything perfectly. Consequently academics tend to focus attention on certain chosen areas for their own career development. Early in an academic career, or when an academic is more experienced but feels in a rut, the annual work review gives them the opportunity to think and talk about trying out a new field or developing new skills. Like any apprentice-ship scheme, the aim should be to get some experience in as many elements of higher education activity as possible – but to focus on one area of develop-ment at a time and find out which holds the most interest.

Those who have come into higher education from a traditional research student/post doctoral research background might try out some enterprise activity one year, or be a year tutor and focus on student support. Those from another professional background might be interested in higher education administration. They might volunteer to be departmental representative on a quality or research ethics committee, or take responsibility for assessment co-ordination. Other options are to develop research skills, undertake a re-search degree or become a junior member of a project team. Trying some-thing new will probably add to the overall workload, but if it suits a career plan then it is better than having a job allocated on the basis of Buggins' turn!

If the new role is enjoyable it is a chance to develop knowledge and skills in the field. If it does not work out, the next annual review is an opportunity to make a change. Many heads of department are not trained personnel managers: whilst they have to balance the needs of the department and individuals, they usually want staff to be proactive about their work and career planning. Colleagues can also be a source of advice about what they do and the chal-lenges and joys of their roles.

Academics who teach part-time or who are paid on an hourly basis might find it difficult to take on additional responsibilities: they are unlikely to be paid for the time needed and people may feel uncomfortable at allocating unpaid work. But they might undertake short courses in teaching techniques or become a module leader, giving them more control over what happens in the teaching, as well enhancing their CV.

However, many people like their job as it is and continue in the same role for many years; the challenges posed by original research and the changing nature of the curriculum and the student body keep the job fresh. The future, though, may be another country. Understanding what is shaping it and how it impacts on our work and roles is critical for our effectiveness and efficiency. Keeping abreast of constant change means not perpetually having to run to keep up.

Future shock/Future proofing

Alvin Toffler, who coined the term 'future shock', was asked in an interview what had led him to the view that society was being torn apart by 'the premature arrival of the future' (Toffler, 1970:17). His response resonates with our experience in higher education today.

> While covering Congress, it occurred to us that big technological and social changes were occurring in the United States, but that the political system seemed totally blind to their existence. Between 1955 and 1960, the birth control pill was introduced, television became universalized [sic], commercial jet travel came into being and a whole raft of other technological events occurred. Having spent several years watching the political process, we came away feeling that 99 per cent of what politicians do is keep systems running that were laid in place by previous generations of politicians. (*New Scientist*, 1994)

Toffer explained how nostalgia for how things used to be done encourages people to search for solutions in past ideas and behaviour – a fruitless approach.

Many of the dilemmas we face could be due to our own 'future shock' experience. This book has explored the social, political and economic changes which have impacted on universities – on the student body, the channels we use for teaching and learning, the ways we communicate between ourselves and with our public, and the tools with which we seek to advance knowledge and understanding.

At the time of writing, the Open University has just held its annual Learning and Technology conference entirely online for the first time. Over two days, synchronous presentations were held in Elluminate (a web-conferencing programme allowing virtual classrooms or meeting spaces) and asynchronous discussions in Cloudworks (a social networking site developed by the OU for finding, sharing and discussing learning and teaching ideas and designs). The conference was open access and, instead of paper contributions, web format items such as Youtube or Slideshare were requested. This may have been exciting and challenging for some but others will regard it as a technological step too far – yet another thing to have to learn about.

We opened this book with two questions: what is meant by higher education in the 21st century and what is the role of an academic in this context? We have tried to describe and explain the context and advise how one might operate within it. We pointed out that in spite of some continuities, change has been persistent. But the extent to which the continuities are essential components of the HE system or a consequence of the reification of custom and practice is still open to debate. We all need to participate in that debate.

We cannot predict the future for higher education, nor the shape, size and characteristics of the future academic role. But by understanding the context and relating practice to it, readers can, to some extent, future proof themselves. Lifelong learning is not only something we need to equip our students for. We, too, need to pursue it in order to ensure that higher education continues to challenge in every way.

Useful Links

Academic-related mailing lists in the UK: http://www.jiscmail.ac.uk

Association for Learning Technology: http://www.alt.ac.uk/

Belbin Team roles: http://www.belbin.com/belbin-team-roles.htm

Colorado State University guidance on forming a self-selecting group: http://writing.colostate.edu/guides/processes/group/list9.cfm/

Destination of Leavers from Higher Education http://dlhe.hesa.ac.uk/

Equality Challenge Unit: http://www.ecu.ac.uk/

Film and sound clips for use in HE: http://www.filmandsound.ac.uk/

HEA Subject centres: http://www.heacademy.ac.uk/subjectcentres

HEA: http://www.eacademy.ac.uk/

Higher Education Funding Council for England: www.hefce.ac.uk

Higher Education Policy Institute: www.hepi.ac.uk

Higher Education Statistics Agency: www.hesa.ac.uk

Image repository: http://www.freeimages.co.uk/

Image Search engine: http://images.google.co.uk

Internet resource training suite: http://www.vts.intute.ac.uk

JISC advisory service on accessibility and inclusion in technology, http://www.techdis.ac.uk/

JISC digital media advice: http://www.tasi.ac.uk/

Multimedia Resource for Learning and Online Teaching : http://www.merlot.org/

National Co-ordinating Centre for Public Engagement : http://www.publicengagement.ac.uk/

National Institute for Health Research: http://www.rdinfo.org.uk/

Photograph repository: http://www.flickr.com/

Photograph repository: http://www.freedigitalphotos.net/

QAA: http://www.qaa.ac.uk/

Research Councils UK: http://www.rcuk.ac.uk/

Research funding and information updates: http://www.researchresearch.com

Twitter: http://www.twitter.com

UCAS: http://www.ucas.ac.uk/

UK Funding bodies: England http://www.hefce.ac.uk/, Wales http://www.hefcw.ac.uk/, Scotland http://www.sfc.ac.uk/, Northern Ireland http://www.delni.gov.uk

UK Joint Information Systems committee: http://www.jisc.ac.uk

UK teaching materials repository: http://www.jorum.ac.uk

Voting systems for lectures: http://www.keele.org.uk/cubes/

References

Anderson, L. W., and Krathwohl, D. R. (Eds.) (2001) *A taxonomy for learning, teaching and assessing: A revision of Bloom's Taxonomy of educational objectives: Complete edition*. New York, Longman.

Arthur, L. (2009) 'From performativity to professionalism: lecturers' responses to student feedback.' *Teaching in Higher Education* 14(4): 441-454.

Attwood, R. (2007) Rammell hails business input in skills-gap battle. *The Times Higher Education Supplement*.

Banks, D. (2006) *Audience response systems in higher education: Applications and cases*, Information Science Publishing.

Barnett, R. (1990) *The Idea of Higher Education*. Maidenhead, SRHE/Open University Press.

Becher, T. and P. R. Trowler (2001) *Academic Tribes and Territories*. Maidenhead, SRHE/Open University Press.

Bekhradnia, B. (2007) 'Demand for Higher Education to 2020 and beyond.' Retrieved May 2010, from http://www.hepi.ac.uk/466-1299/Demand-for-Higher-Education-to-2020-and-beyond.html.

Bell, D. (1973) *The Coming of Post-industrial Society*. New York, Basic Books.

Bennett, R., L. Eagle, *et al.* (2008) 'Reassessing the value of work-experience placements in the context of widening participation in higher education.' *Journal of Vocational Education and Training* 60(2): 105-122.

Biggs, J. (2003, 10/11/2006 16:20:43) 'Aligning teaching for constructing learning.' Retrieved 08/04/09, 2009, from http://www.heacademy.ac.uk/resources/detail/id477_aligning_teaching_for_constructing_learning.

Biggs, J. and C. Tang (2007) *Teaching for Quality Learning at University* (3rd Ed), Open University Press.

BIS (2009) *Higher Ambitions*. London, Department for Business, Innovation and Skills.

Bligh, D. (2000) *What's the Use of Lectures?* San Francisco, Jossey-Bass.

Bloom, B. (1956) *Taxonomy of Educational Objectives: The Classification of Educational Goals*, Susan Fauer Company, Inc.

Bostock, S., J. Hulme, *et al.* (2006) 'Communicubes: intermediate technology for interaction with student groups.' Audience response systems in higher education, applications and cases. Hershey, PA: *Information Science Publishing*: 321-333.

Boud, D. (1995) Assessment and Learning: contradictory or complementary? in P. Knight *Assessment for Learning in Higher Education*. London, Kogan Page: 35-48.

Brown, S. and P. Race (2002) *Lecturing: A Practical Guide*, Taylor and Francis.

Cohen, R. and P. Kennedy (2000) *Global sociology*. Basingstoke, Macmillan.

Committee on Higher Education (1963) *Robbins Report*. London.

Cook, A., B. S. Rushton, *et al* (2005) *Guidelines for the Management of Student Transition.* Ulster, STAR project, University of Ulster.

Coomes, M. and R. DeBard (2004) 'A generational approach to understanding students.' *New Directions for Student Services* 2004(106): 5-16.

Dawson, M., C. Ainley, *et al.* (2009) The MMU First Year 'Shock Absorber' project. Science Learning and Teaching Conference 2009, Heriot-Watt University, Edinburgh.

Dearing, R. (1997) *Report of the National Committee of Inquiry into Higher Education.* London, HMG.

Ecclestone, K. (2001) "I know a 2:1 when I see it': understanding criteria for degree classifications in franchise university programmes.' *Journal of Further and Higher Education* 25(3): 301-312.

European Education Ministers. (1999) 'Bologna Declaration.' Retrieved May 2010, from http://www.ond.vlaanderen.be/hogeronderwijs/bologna/documents/MDC/BOLOGNA_DECLARATION1.pdf.

Friedman, T. (2000) *The Lexus and the olive tree.* New York, Farrar, Straus and Giroux.

Furedi, F. (2003) Children Who Won't Grow Up. Retrieved May 2010, from http://www.spiked-online.com/index.php/site/article/2775/.

Giddens, A. (1990) *The Consequences of Modernity.* Cambridge, Polity.

Graham, G. (2002) *Universities: the Recovery of an Idea.* Charlottesville, Imprint Academic.

Graham, G. (2005) *The institution of intellectual values: Realism and idealism in higher education.* Charlottesville, Imprint Academic.

Handal, G. (2008) Identities of Academic Developers: Critical Friends in the Academy? in R. Barnett and R. DiNapoli (eds). *Changing identities in higher education: voicing perspectives.* Abingdon, Routledge.

Hanlon, J., M. Jefferson, *et al.* (2004) Exploring comparative marking. Retrieved May 2010, 2007, from http://www.ukcle.ac.uk/research/projects/mitchell.rtf.

Hawker, S. and J. Elliot, Eds. (2005) *Pocket Oxford English Dictionary,* 10th Edition. Oxford, OUP.

HEFCE. (2008) Funding higher education in England. Retrieved May 2010, 2010, from http://www.hefce.ac.uk/pubs/hefce/2008/08_33/.

HEFCE. (2008) Funding higher education in England: How HEFCE allocates its funds. Retrieved May 2010, from http://www.hefce.ac.uk/pubs/hefce/2008/08_33/.

Hinds, P., K. Carley, *et al.* (2000) 'Choosing work group members: Balancing similarity, competence, and familiarity.' *Organizational Behavior and Human Decision Processes* 81(2): 226-251.

Humboldt, W. (1970) 'On the spirit and organisational framework of intellectual institutions in Berlin.' *Minerva* 8(2): 242-250.

Jones, C., Ramanu, R., Cross, S. and Healing, G. (2010) Net Generation or Digital Natives: is there a distinct new generation entering university? *Computers and Education,* 54(3): 722-732.

Kennedy, H. (1997) *Learning works.* Coventry: Further Education Funding Council.

Knight, P. T. and M. Yorke (2003) *Assessment, Learning and Employability,* SRHE/OUP.

Langan, D. A. M. and D. C. P. Wheater (2003) 'Can students assess students effectively? Some insights into peer-assessment.' *Learning and Teaching in Action* 2(1)

LeCourt, D. and D. Kowalski. (2010) Working in Groups. Retrieved 30/09/10, 2010.

Leitch, S. (2006) *Prosperity for all in the global economy – world class skills,* HM Treasury.

Liu, N.-F. and D. Carless (2006) 'Peer feedback: the learning element of peer assessment.' *Teaching in Higher Education* 11(3): 279-290.

Longden, B. (2006) 'An Institutional response to changing student expectations and their impact on retention rates.' *Journal of Higher Education Policy and Management* 28(2): 173-187.

REFERENCES

Mannheim, K. (1952) *The problem of generations: Essays on the sociology of knowledge.* Kecskemeti. London.

Maskell, D. and I. Robinson (2002) *The New Idea of a University.* Charlottesville, Imprint Academic.

McLuhan, M. (1964) *Understanding media: the extension of man.* New York, McGraw Hill.

MMU (2009) *Framework for the management of student transition and induction.* Manchester, Manchester Metropolitan University.

NCIHE. (1997) Higher Education in the Learning Society. Retrieved May 2010, from http://www.leeds.ac.uk/educol/ncihe/.

New Scientist (1994) Alvin Toffler: still shocking after all these years. *New Scientist.* 22-25.

Newman, J. (1854) *What is a University.* Salt Lake City, Project Gutenberg.

Nicol, D. and D. Macfarlane, Debra (2006) 'Formative assessment and self-regulated learning: a model and seven principles of good feedback practice.' *Studies in Higher Education* 31(2): 199-218.

OECD (2009) *OECD Science, Technology and Industry Scoreboard Highlights 2009.* Paris, OECD Directorate for Science Technology and Industry.

Prowse, S., N. Duncan, *et al.* (2007) '..... do that and I'll raise your grade'. Innovative module design and recursive feedback. *Teaching in Higher Education* 12(4): 437-445.

QAA. (2006) Code of practice for the assurance of academic quality and standards in higher education. 2. Retrieved 28/05/08, 2008, from http://www.qaa.ac.uk/academicinfrastructure/code OfPractice/section6/default.asp.

Race, P. (2005) *Making Learning Happen: A guide for Post-Compulsory Education,* Sage.

Race, P. and R. Pickford (2007) *Making Teaching Work: Teaching Smarter in Post-Compulsory Education,* Sage Publications Ltd.

Ramsden, B. (2006) *Patterns of higher education institutions in the UK: Sixth report.* London, UUK.

Redmond, P. (2007) *'Talking 'bout my generation:' the role of Generation Theory in understanding students' attitudes to careers and employability.* ARN symposium, Manchester.

Redmond, P. (2008a) Generation Y: Maximising the value of generations in the 21st century workplace.' Retrieved September 2009, from http://staffdev.ulster.ac.uk/uploads/Paul%20 Redmond.ppt.

Redmond, P. (2008b) Here Comes the Chopper. *The Guardian,* 2 January.

Rowland, S. (2006) *The Enquiring University: Compliance and contestation in higher education.* Maidenhead, McGraw Hill.

Salmon, G. (2002) *e-tivities,* Kogan Page.

Scott, P. (1995) *The Meanings of Mass Higher Education.* Bristol, Open University Press.

Slaughter, S. and L. L. Leslie (1997) *Academic Capitalism: Politics, Policies, and the Entrepreneurial University.* Baltimore, The Johns Hopkins University Press.

Stead, D. R. (2005) 'A review of the one-minute paper.' *Active Learning in Higher Education* 6(2): 118-131.

Strauss, W. and N. Howe (1991) *Generations,* Morrow.

Toffler, A. (1970) *Future Shock.* London, The Bodley Head Ltd.

Trow, M. (1973) Problems in the transition from elite to mass high education in Policies for Higher Education, from the General Report on the Conference in Future Students of Post-Secondary Education, Paris: OECD.

Universities UK. (2008) 'The higher education sector and UK universities.' Retrieved May 2010, 2010, from http://www.universitiesuk.ac.uk/UKHESector/FAQs/Pages/About-HE-Sector-and-Universities.aspx.

Waters, M. (1995) *Globalization: Key Ideas,* London: Routledge.

Watson, D. (2008) Who owns the university? A QAA briefing paper. Retrieved May 2010, 2010, from http://www.qaa.ac.uk/aboutus/contactus.asp.

Webster, F. (1995) *Theories of the information society.* New York, Routledge.

Whitton, N., S. Wilson, *et al.* (2008) Innovative induction with Alternate Reality Games. 2nd European Conference on Game-Based Learning, Barcelona.

Yorke, M., P. Bridges, *et al.* (2000) 'Mark Distributions and Marking Practices in UK Higher Education.' *Active Learning in Higher Education* 1(1): 7-27.

Yorke, M. and B. Longden (2007) *The first-year experience in higher education in the UK*, Higher Education Academy.

Index